Words of Wisdom
A N D   K N O W L E D G E

— for —

ORDINARY PEOPLE
with an extraordinary gift

Words of Wisdom
AND KNOWLEDGE

— *for* —

Prophetic PEOPLE

ORDINARY PEOPLE
with an extraordinary gift

Wilbur **DANIEL**

Roanoke Rapids, NC

Unless otherwise indicated, all Scripture are taken from the King James Version of the Holy Bible.

Words of Wisdom & Knowledge for Prophetic People
First Edition

Library of Congress Control Number: 2011911360

ISBN 10: 0-61551-799-4 (paperback)
ISBN-13: 978-0-615-51799-5 (paperback)

Printed in the United States of America

Copyright © 2011 by Wilbur Daniel
All rights reserved

Published by WDM
Wilbur Daniel Ministries

Cover Design
Illustrations & Page Formatting
by Wilbur Daniel
Edited By Kimberley A. Robinson

No part of this publication may be reproduced, stored in a retrieval system, or transmitted in any form or by any means-electronic, mechanical, photocopying, recording, or otherwise-without the prior written permission of the publisher and copyright owner.

For additional information visit
www.wilburdaniel.com

Table of Contents

Dedication..	9
Acknowledgments...................................	10
Introduction...	11
The vision..	12

Session One   Prophetic Order & Structure (13)

Grace...	14
You Didn't Get Where You Are Overnight........	15
God Ordered Course................................	16
The Discovery Process.............................	17
The Process..	18
It's Not You It's The Anointing.................	19, 20
Who Can God Use...................................	21, 22
I Have Chosen And Ordained You............	23
Among The Elect.....................................	24
God's Government..................................	25
God's Spiritual Responsibility..................	26, 27
You're Here For A Reason........................	28
Preserved For Purpose............................	29
The Work of Ministry..............................	30
Protocol of A Minister.............................	31
Different Kinds of Ministries...................	32
Personal Ministry...................................	33

Table of Contents

| Session Two | Prophecy | 35 |

Prophecy..	36
Confirmation..	37
Prophecy Is Conditional..	39
9 Gifts of The Spirit..	40
Word of knowledge..	41
Discerning of Spirits...	42
Realms of Prophecy..	43
The Source of Revelation...	44
Ro'eh...	45
Chozeh..	46
Rhema Word..	47
Dabar...	48,49
Decreeing..	50
Declaring...	50
Know Your Season..	51
God's Pre-Written Book of Your Life..................................	52
The Creative Spoken Word...	53
The Creative Spoken Word of The Lord............................	54
The Creative Spoken Word of The Prophet......................	55,57
Dreams..	58,59
Other Than God Know That You're In Control..................	60
Inner Council of The Lord..	61
Insight, Foresight And Vision..	62

Table of Contents

Session Three	Prophets	**65**
Different Kinds of Prophets		66
Why Prophets		67
Modern Day Prophets		68
A Must		69
The Lord Establishes The Prophet		70,71
Every Prophet Must Be Time Proven		72
Prophets Must Be Broken		73
Office of The Prophet		74,75
In God's Care		76
God Brought you Out		77
Ministry		78
Ministry of The Prophet		79,80
The Prophet's Message		81
Prophets Prepare The Way of the Lord		82
5 Major Prophets		84
12 Minor Prophets		85
Knowing Your Own Company		86,87
The SEED Group		88,89
Samuel		90,93
Samuel Anoints Saul		94,95
Elijah		96,97
Elisha		98,99
Daniel		100,101

Session Four	School of The Prophets	**103**
The Origin		104
Wisdom		105
How To Receive A Prophet		106-110
Guidelines For Prophesying		111
Fed By God		112
When God Wins Your Confidence		113
When It's Time God Will Have Then Send For You		114
The Prophetic Minstrel Ushers In The Spirit of The Lord		115

Table of Contents

Session Five — Prophets And Prosperity — 117

Prophets And Prosperity	118
It's God That Prospers You	119
Whatever God Speaks	120
Don't Re-Invent The Wheel	121
Back Into It Step By Step	122, 123
You Already Have What You Are Looking For	124
Is It For Now Or Later	127
The Law of Reciprocity	128
God Never Promotes You Past Your Last Assignment	129
A Prophet Must Understand The Seasons And Times	130, 131

Session Six — Prophets & Spiritual Warfare — 133

What Is Spiritual Warfare	134
God Will Shut The Lions Mouth	135
Pushed Into The Hands of God	137
Know Your Strengths And Weakness	138
The Power of Prayer	139
Inner Council of the Lord	140-141
The Spirit Realm	142
What A Prophet Does He Must Do In The Spirit	143
The Law of The Spirit	144,147
Fear Not	148
Release A Creative Word Over Your Life	149
Open Doors	150
Jealousy A Vision Killer	151
Depression It Comes After Victory	152
Don't Be Dismayed At Their Faces	153
Hidden By God	154
God's Way of Getting You Out	155
When God Opens Your Eyes	156
God Bless The Real You	157
Let It Go	159

Dedication

To the Lord Jesus Christ, who gave me the wisdom and knowledge to live and experience this book. Thank you Lord Jesus.

To my wife, Charmaine, my two grandchildren, Carlos and Jasmine. My daughters, Alexandria and Charisma, who one day will carry the mantle that's upon my life.

To all the young budding prophets and prophetess and prophetic people. May this book help you on your journey to maturity.

To my immediate family, and church family, my brothers and sisters in Christ.

Prophet Wilbur Daniel
July 30, 2011

Acknowledgments

    I acknowledge the Holy Spirit for the revelation knowledge, wisdom, counsel and understanding that He revealed to me from my Father God.

    I acknowledge my wife Charmaine Daniel my two daughters, Alexandria and Charisma my sister Melissa and her husband Art Bechhoefer for the time, inspiration and contributions they gave for me to write this book.

Thank you family.

Introduction

This is not just another book on the prophetic with lots of words and prophetic terms that you may not understand. This book is based on a few of Wilbur Daniel's real life experiences, as a budding prophet being developed by God. Before prophets are officially released by God, He takes every budding prophet through a process of development, some are different from others. Written in this book are some of the main principles and words of wisdom you will experience as a budding prophet. Budding prophets need to be taught, activated and matured, to be responsible and effective prophetic team members in the service of the Lord Jesus Christ, making people ready for the Lord's second return.

Jesus according to *Ephesians 4:11* gave purpose to the fivefold extension gifts when he ascended up on high, His main purpose for coming to earth was to seek out and to save those who were lost. This prophetic book is another tool God desires to use in the earth, to help educate those who are prophetically lost due to zeal without knowledge, improper teaching, and a lack of platforms to express themselves under the proper covering; leadership that doesn't understand the prophetic; false prophets that have corrupted the office; and most of all religion and tradition of men.

You are about to enter into prophetic zone of wisdom, information and real life experiences that took Wilbur Daniel five years to write. This book contains life markers that you can relate to and may have already have experienced.

THE VISION

Habakkuk 2:1-4

The Beauty it Beholds

- If you don't write it, they can't run with it

- If they can't run with it, they can't build it

- If they can't build it, they don't come

- If they don't come they perish

- If they perish, they are unfulfilled

- If they are unfulfilled you're accountable

- If you're accountable you'll be judged

- If you be judged

THEN WHAT ?

training prophetic people to develop a strong clear prophetic flow

Session One
Prophetic Order & Structure

GRACE

> Grace is the free unmerited favor of GOD. I didn't do anything for GOD to create all these things for me before I was born. Things are tools, because all things are tools and can be of service in some way whether old or new. Tools have features which give you options in service that allow you to have different compatibilities. Grace says that it's in place, complete finished. GOD created the earth and put everything in it that I needed. Grace is the dominion that you function in. Faith is what you use to access it and wisdom and knowledge are what you use to keep it, after you have obtained it.

——— Wilbur Daniel

Eph 2:8-10 (KJV)

8 For by grace are ye saved through faith; and that not of yourselves: it is the gift of God:
9 Not of works, lest any man should boast.
10 For we are his workmanship, created in Christ Jesus unto good works, which God hath before ordained that we should walk in them.

SESSION ONE  PROPHETIC ORDER & STRUCTURE   15

training prophetic people to develop a strong clear prophetic flow

YOU DIDN'T GET WHERE YOU ARE OVER NIGHT

> Jesus came through 42 generations

Gal 4:4-7

4 But when the fulness of the time was come, God sent forth his Son, made of a woman, made under the law,
5 To redeem them that were under the law, that we might receive the adoption of sons.
6 And because ye are sons, God hath sent forth the Spirit of his Son into your hearts, crying, Abba, Father.
7 Wherefore thou art no more a servant, but a son; and if a son, then an heir of God through Christ.

GOD'S ORDERED COURSE

> The Bible says Samuel traveled in a circuit judging Israel all the days of his life.

1 Sam 7:15-17 (KJV)
15 And Samuel judged Israel all the days of his life.
16 And he went from year to year in circuit to Bethel, and Gilgal, and Mizpeh, and judged Israel in all those places.
17 And his return was to Ramah; for there was his house; and there he judged Israel; and there he built an altar unto the LORD.

The Bible states, Samuel traveled in a circuit judging Israel all the days of his life. After reading a prophetic book on scribal writing the Holy Spirit spoke to me and said, the office that I have set you in, you will function by writing prophetic curriculums and prophetic instructional material, through information that will be gathered from fellowshipping in different Churches. Being in the congregation of my people, the Holy Spirit will show you where the body need to be aligned. As a result, instructional material will be written that will be used to educate believers in their fivefold gifts.

THE DISCOVERY PROCESS

Every God ordained prophet has been assigned a task from the Father whether large or small. Without proper mentoring and guidance, most young prophets will go through a long series of detours which take years from their discover process. Prophets that are mentored properly will or may take a third or half the time to know their assignment.

- Example prophet Moses wondered 4o years in the wilderness before he reached the promise land Cannaan

- Example Elisha was mentored by Elijah and it took him less than 40 years to discover his prophetic task.

Elisha walked with Elijah and served him, when the time came for Elijah to be taken up, the mantle was passed to Elisha. From serving so close to his master Elisha the young prophet knew what to do, not only did he know what to do, God also gave him his own assignment, which he was capable of accomplishing from serving Elijah.

EACH PROPHET PROCESS OF DISCOVERY WILL BE DIFFERENT

THE PROCESS

> Every prophet must be processed by God

1. It may be Daniel in the lions den.
   (Daniel 6:16)

2. Jonah's experience in the fish.
   (Jonah 1:17)

3. Moses with the back side of the desert.
   (Exodus 3:1)

4. or you with your experience

IT'S NOT YOU...
IT'S THE ANOINTING

The old spiritual song writer sang, "without God I would be nothing, without God I would fail, without God my life would be drifted just like a ship without a sail".

The anointing is like the wind that blows into the sail. The anointing propels us. Sails on ships are the power source that causes a ship to move after the wind is blown into it. The anointing is what breaks and destroys the yoke.

> *Isaiah 10:27-28 (KJV)*
> *27 And it shall come to pass in that day, that his burden shall be taken away from off thy shoulder, and his yoke from off thy neck, and the yoke shall be destroyed because of the anointing. 28 He is come to Aiath, he is passed to Migron; at Michmash he hath laid up his carriages:*

The anointing is the endorsement power that one functions in to destroy the yoke. The anointing, the enabling endorsement power comes from God.

SESSION ONE   PROPHECTIC ORDER & STRUCTURE

training prophetic people to develop a strong clear prophetic flow

IT'S NOT YOU...
IT'S THE ANOINTING

> When Jesus came to Jerusalem on the donkey and people began to say, "Hosanna, Hosanna," the donkey could have easily thought they were cheering him on. Don't get it twisted, when you're getting cheers remember it's not you, it's the anointing on you.

Mark 11:7-9 (KJV)
7 And they brought the colt to Jesus, and cast their garments on him; and he sat upon him.
8 And many spread their garments in the way: and others cut down branches off the trees, and strawed them in the way.
9 And they that went before, and they that followed, cried, saying, Hosanna; Blessed is he that cometh in the name of the Lord:

When the spirit of the Lord came upon Samson he was able to slay a thousand men with the single jawbone of a jackass, you become as another man when the anointing come upon you.

Judges 15:15-16 (KJV)
15 And he found a new jawbone of an ass, and put forth his hand, and took it, and slew a thousand men therewith.
16 And Samson said, With the jawbone of an ass, heaps upon heaps, with the jaw of an ass have I slain a thousand men.

WHO CAN GOD USE

WHO CAN GOD USE ?
- Anyone that yields themselves to Him
- How can you yield yourself to God?
- In all thy ways acknowledge Him. *Proverbs 3:6*

God uses all kinds of people and people use all kinds of things on the earth. Everyone and everything we need is in the earth, seek it out and pray to the Father that he may direct you to it or them. *Psalms 37:23 (KJV)*

- Seek and you shall find, knock and the door shall be open, ask and it shall be given *Luke 11:9 (KJV)*

- Solomon - Sought out wisdom and the understanding of things. *Ecclesiastes 12:9-10 (KJV)*

- Professional people - Doctors they use surgery - tools, scissors, scalpel,
- Lawyers - Use cases, information,
- Scientist - Experiments with microscope
- Preachers - Uses God's Word, spoken Word, Bible and faith,
- Dentists - Uses needles, pliers, x-rays and novocaine.
- Bankers - Uses loans and money

What kind of things do people use?

- Prayer - Prayer directs us directly to God. God then can direct us to the exact people that have the right things we need.
- Tools • Computers • Cars • Etc.

Holy Spirit

Jesus

God the Father
Revelation knowledge
Wisdom, Counsel, Power, Riches,

(Surrounded by: Jesus / Holy Spirit on all sides)

Holy Spirit

Revelation knowledge comes from the Father, by the Holy Spirit.

God uses man's
Spiritual Gifts, Natural Gifts, Talents & Skills

God uses man & man uses things
There are two type of people
People with needs - Needing services or products (things)
People that fulfill needs - through services or products (things)

Pray to the Father
Ask him to direct you to the exact person that can fulfill your need, by way of service or product.

To fulfill both people
There must be a mutual exchange of service or product, that exchange can be rendered in many different ways,
• Blessings • Favor • Business • Loans • Gifts • Etc.

Below are different people that provide a service or product
Prophets, Preachers, Doctors, Lawyers, Artist, Brokers, and Bankers,

Man with a need
Artwork, Counsel, etc.
Exchange: Money for time, talent and service.

Goal of Exchange

Men that fulfills needs with service or product
Artist, Counselor, etc.
computer graphics, prophecy

SESSION ONE  **PROPHECTIC ORDER & STRUCTURE**

training prophetic people to develop a strong clear prophetic flow

I HAVE CHOSEN AND ORDAINED YOU

> One Monday night around 9:00 pm, the Word of the Lord came to me and said," I have chosen you and ordained you to go and bring forth fruit that will remain."

16 Ye have not chosen me, but I have chosen you, and ordained you, that ye should go and bring forth fruit, and that your fruit should remain: that whatsoever ye shall ask of the Father in my name, he may give it you.

John 15:16 (KJV)
Exodus 16:15-20 (KJV)

SESSION ONE  PROPHECTIC ORDER & STRUCTURE

training prophetic people to develop a strong clear prophetic flow

AMONG THE ELECT

> Jesus in the midst of the doctors.

Luke 2:40-49

40 And the child grew, and waxed strong in spirit, filled with wisdom: and the grace of God was upon him.
41 Now his parents went to Jerusalem every year at the feast of the passover.
42 And when he was twelve years old, they went up to Jerusalem after the custom of the feast.
43 And when they had fulfilled the days, as they returned, the child Jesus tarried behind in Jerusalem; and Joseph and his mother knew not of it.
44 But they, supposing him to have been in the company, went a day's journey; and they sought him among their kinsfolk and acquaintance.
45 And when they found him not, they turned back again to Jerusalem, seeking him.
46 And it came to pass, that after three days they found him in the temple, sitting in the midst of the doctors, both hearing them, and asking them questions.
47 And all that heard him were astonished at his understanding and answers.
48 And when they saw him, they were amazed: and his mother said unto him, Son, why hast thou thus dealt with us? behold, thy father and I have sought thee sorrowing.
49 And he said unto them, How is it that ye sought me? wist ye not that I must be about my Father's business?

GOD'S GOVERNMENT
FOR THE KINGDOM

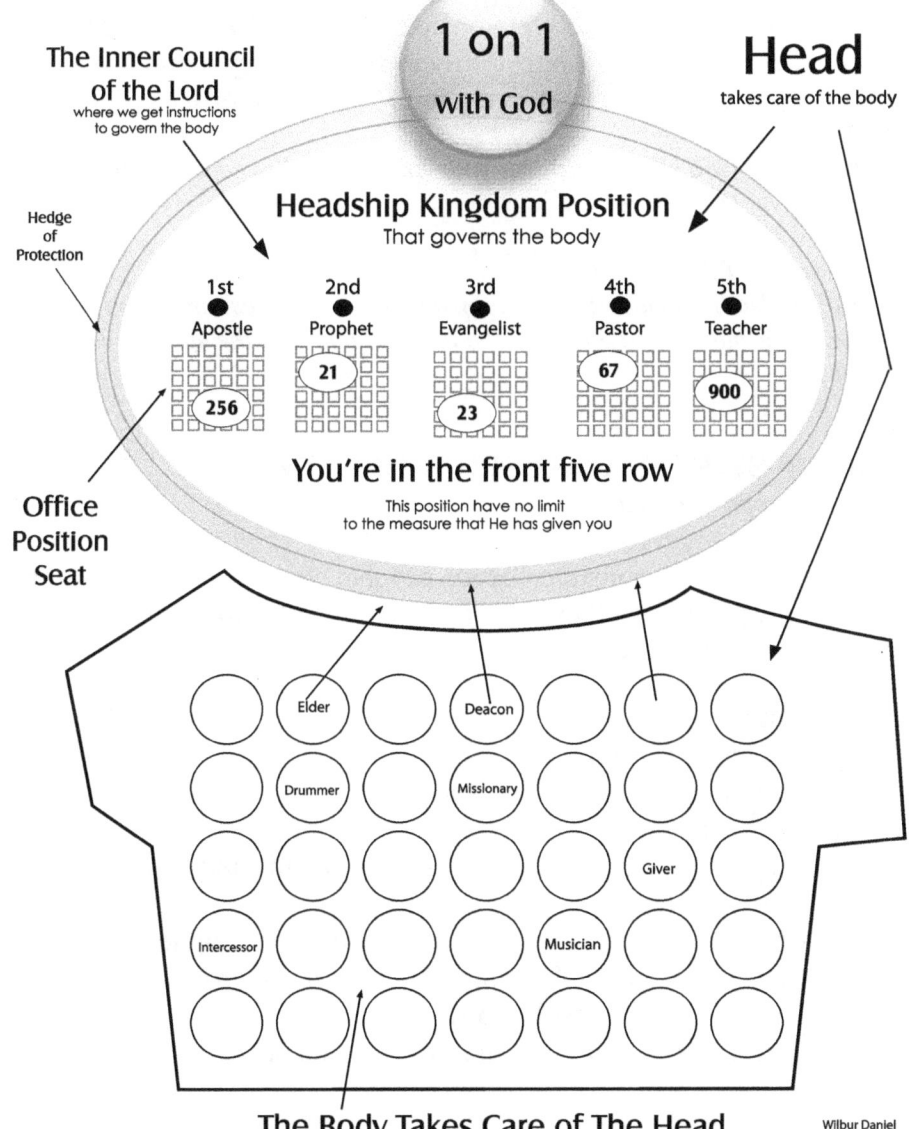

RESPONSIBILITY

GOD'S SPIRITUAL RESPONSIBILITY
to the prophet/prophetess

Once God choose you and set you apart into the office of the prophet/prophetess, it's His responsibility to supply every natural tool you need to function effectively in the prophetic office.

Phil 4:19 (KJV)
19 But my God shall supply all your need according to his riches in glory by Christ Jesus.

2 Cor 3:6 (KJV)
6 Who also hath made us able ministers of the new testament; not of the letter, but of the spirit: for the letter killeth, but the spirit giveth life.

GOD'S SPIRITUAL RESPONSIBILITY
to the prophet/prophetess

God is totally responsible for all prophet's/prophetess natural and spiritual provisions they need to function with and fulfill their God given calling and mission.

- Revelation Knowledge
- Visions, dreams, trances
- Measure of anointing and power
- Spiritual wisdom
- Mystery of the Word of God - Paul said the mystery was given to him by revelation.
- Direct Word to the people - Go to Nineveh and prophesy
- Inspiration to write - Old men in ancient times wrote as they were inspired by the Holy Spirit.
- To open doors - A door of utterance may be open.

RESPONSIBILITY

GOD'S NATURAL RESPONSIBILITY
to the prophet/prophetss

God is responsible for all the prophet's/prophetess' natural provisions they need to function with and fulfill their God given calling and mission. Jesus said greater works shall you do.

BC/AD time period that the prophets and Jesus lived in didn't have the technology to work ministry that we have in 2009. Greater works are clearly defined by advancing ministry through technology, media and other material.

Example: *Where it may have taken Jonah three days to travel through Ninevah on foot, wagon or animals. The greater work I believe Jesus referred to is, the three days it may have taken Jonah in his period by foot or other means of transportation, now only take us a fews hours by a vehicle or plane, etc. - Wilbur Daniel*

> *12 Verily, verily, I say unto you, He that believeth on me, the works that I do shall he do also; and greater works than these shall he do; because I go unto my Father.*
> *13 And whatsoever ye shall ask in my name, that will I do, that the Father may be glorified in the Son.*
> *14 If ye shall ask any thing in my name, I will do it.*
> *John 14:12-14 (KJV)*

GOD'S NATURAL RESPONSIBLE
to the prophet/prophetess

The fivefold office that the Father God has placed you in, requires a certain level of natural substance, tools and material to effectively do greater works in ministry for the time period that you are assigned.

SESSION ONE  PROPHECTIC ORDER & STRUCTURE

training prophetic people to develop a strong clear prophetic flow

YOU'RE HERE FOR A REASON

> Joseph was sold to Potiphar for an appointed time, to preserve his people during the famine.

Gen 37:28

Then there passed by Midianites merchantmen; and they drew and lifted up Joseph out of the pit, and sold Joseph to the Ishmeelites for twenty pieces of silver: and they brought Joseph into Egypt.

PRESERVED FOR PURPOSE

> Esther was preserved for a time when all the Jewish people were about to be vanished. God allowed her to come forth for such a time to save her people from extinction. For what purpose is He preserving you?
>
> —— *Wilbur Daniel*

Esther 8:4-6

4 Then the king held out the golden sceptre toward Esther. So Esther arose, and stood before the king,
5 And said, If it please the king, and if I have found favour in his sight, and the thing seem right before the king, and I be pleasing in his eyes, let it be written to reverse the letters devised by Haman the son of Hammedatha the Agagite, which he wrote to destroy the Jews which are in all the king's provinces:
6 For how can I endure to see the evil that shall come unto my people? or how can I endure to see the destruction of my kindred?

THE WORK *of* MINISTRY

The work of ministry is a religious and spiritual service to the general public.

Acts 6:1-7 (KJV)
1 And in those days, when the number of the disciples was multiplied, there arose a murmuring of the Grecians against the Hebrews, because their widows were neglected in the daily ministration.
2 Then the twelve called the multitude of the disciples unto them, and said, It is not reason that we should leave the word of God, and serve tables.
3 Wherefore, brethren, look ye out among you seven men of honest report, full of the Holy Ghost and wisdom, whom we may appoint over this business.
4 But we will give ourselves continually to prayer, and to the ministry of the word.
5 And the saying pleased the whole multitude: and they chose Stephen, a man full of faith and of the Holy Ghost, and Philip, and Prochorus, and Nicanor, and Timon, and Parmenas, and Nicolas a proselyte of Antioch:
6 Whom they set before the apostles: and when they had prayed, they laid their hands on them.
7 And the word of God increased; and the number of the disciples multiplied in Jerusalem greatly; and a great company of the priests were obedient to the faith.

1 Tim 1:12 (KJV)
12 And I thank Christ Jesus our Lord, who hath enabled me, for that he counted me faithful, putting me into the ministry;

PROTOCOL *of* A MINISTER

Mark 10:35-45 (KJV)
35 And James and John, the sons of Zebedee, come unto him, saying, Master, we would that thou shouldest do for us whatsoever we shall desire.
36 And he said unto them, What would ye that I should do for you?
37 unto him, Grant unto us that we may sit, one on thy right hand, and the other on thy left hand, in thy glory.
38 But Jesus said unto them, Ye know not what ye ask: can ye drink of the cup that I drink of? and be baptized with the baptism that I am baptized with?
39 And they said unto him, We can. And Jesus said unto them, Ye shall indeed drink of the cup that I drink of; and with the baptism that I am baptized withal shall ye be baptized:
40 But to sit on my right hand and on my left hand is not mine to give; but it shall be given to them for whom it is prepared.
41 And when the ten heard it, they began to be much displeased with James and John.
42 But Jesus called them to him, and saith unto them, Ye know that they which are accounted to rule over the Gentiles exercise lordship over them; and their great ones exercise authority upon them.

43 But so shall it not be among you: but whosoever will be great among you, shall be your minister:

44 And whosoever of you will be the chiefest, shall be servant of all.
45 For even the Son of man came not to be ministered unto, but to minister, and to give his life a ransom for many.

Different kind of ministries

1 I beseech you therefore, brethren, by the mercies of God, that ye present your bodies a living sacrifice, holy, acceptable unto God, which is your reasonable service.
2 And be not conformed to this world: but be ye transformed by the renewing of your mind, that ye may prove what is that good, and acceptable, and perfect, will of God.
3 For I say, through the grace given unto me, to every man that is among you, not to think of himself more highly than he ought to think; but to think soberly, according as God hath dealt to every man the measure of faith.
4 For as we have many members in one body, and all members have not the same office:
5 So we, being many, are one body in Christ, and every one members one of another.
6 Having then gifts differing according to the grace that is given to us, whether prophecy, let us prophesy according to the proportion of faith;
7 Or ministry, let us wait on our ministering: or he that teacheth, on teaching;
8 Or he that exhorteth, on exhortation: he that giveth, let him do it with simplicity; he that ruleth, with diligence; he that sheweth mercy, with cheerfulness.
9 Let love be without dissimulation. Abhor that which is evil; cleave to that which is good.
Romans 12:1-9 (KJV)

- **Ministry of Helps** - These people aids are an assistant to ministry, their primary ministry is to help where ever they can in local Church.

- **Ministry of the word** - Pastors, Teachers, Philosophers fits this category more than anyone else in the body of Christ. Their life is devoted to research, studying and teaching the Word of God.

PERSONAL MINISTRY

Acts 20:24 (KJV)

24 But none of these things move me, neither count I my life dear unto myself, so that I might finish my course with joy, and the ministry, which I have received of the Lord Jesus, to testify the gospel of the grace of God.

training prophetic people to develop a strong clear prophetic flow

training prophetic people to develop a strong clear prophetic flow

Session Two
Prophecy

PROPHECY

WHAT IS PROPHECY?

Prophecy is divine revelation from God given to a specific individual, that can be communicated in a prophetic mode, to a particular person, group, business, church or individual, for edification, exhortation, comfort and sometime judgment & guidance.

> *Revelation 19:10 (KJV)*
> *And I fell at his feet to worship him. And he said unto me, See thou do it not: I am thy fellowservant, and of thy brethren that have the testimony of Jesus: worship God:*
> ***for the testimony of Jesus is the spirit of prophecy.***
>
> *Revelation 22:16 (KJV)*
> *I Jesus have sent mine angel to testify unto you these things in the churches. I am the root and the offspring of David, and the bright and morning star.*

WHY PROPHECY?

God wants to communicate. He desires intimate fellowship with man rather than a distant relationship with humanity. Humanity is to busy to stop and receive the way He wants to communicate. God wants to communicate to mankind in many different ways:

- Revelation Knowledge
- Visions
- Dreams
- Impressions
- Trances
- The Holy Spirit
- And last but not least his servant the prophet

CONFIRMATION

When certain things are given to you from the Lord by revelation knowledge or vision, ask yourself is it for now or later.

*Write the vision, and make it plain upon tables, that he may run that readeth it. 3 For the vision is yet for an **appointed time**, but at the end it shall speak, and not lie: though it tarry, wait for it; because it will surely come, it will not tarry.*
Hab 2:2-3 (KJV)

Three suggestions **to help determine is it for now or later.**

- By His word
- By His will
- By His way

By His Word
A Rhema Word has been received by prophecy and prophetic preaching also a vision was given with a scripture pertaining to the matter.

By His Will
It's God plan and purpose for you determine by your overall make up. These are things that you would have no spiritual or natural control over. (Example) If God wanted you to be a center basketball player. He would have made you outstanding tall with a desire for basketball.

By His way - You are born into a wealthy family, and your desire is to give millions of dollar to charity.

SESSION TWO — PROPHECY

training prophetic people to develop a strong clear prophetic flow

> God speaks or reveals the word to His servant the prophet. The school of the prophet will come forth. Men and women will come from far and near.

> "The School of the prophets will come forth. Men and women will come from far and near."

The spoken word of the Lord have the power within itself to fulfill itself. Because it's connected with God, who will fulfill that word that he has spoken through His servant the prophet. Immediately after the word of the Lord is spoken the power within it starts to fulfill itself.

Wilbur Daniel

> Prophecy is conditional based upon human responsiblity of obedience to it.

The creative, effecting power in the prophetic word of God is not automatic nor is it unalterably destined to be fulfilled. The prophetic word is conditional upon man's response to the Word of the Lord. Lack of continuous sin, or a pattern of spiritual instability in a believer's life may either delay or entirely block the fulfillment of God's Word.

God does not overstep human responsibility. Although the prophetic word carries the power accomplish that word if unhindered, yet its fulfillment may be hindered by the recipient's life, prophetic word may thus be never fulfilled.

A graphic example of this is the prophecy of Jonah to Nineveh. His message, "Yet forty days and Nineveh shall be overthrown" (Jonah 3:4) was expressed in uncompromising terms. Yet prophecy was obviously conditional, and the prophecy was not fulfilled because of the Nineveh's response.

Some prophetic words in a presbytery will be clearly conditional by the very wording of message. However, those prophetic utterances which are not expressed in conditional must also be considered conditional, for that is God's way of speaking to His people.

> Once the word is Given by God it is the responsibility of the prophet to release it.

9 GIFTS OF THE SPIRIT

ARE DIVIDED INTO 3 CATEGORIES

(1) Voice or vocal gift
- Tongues
- Interpretation of tongues
- Prophecy

(2) Eyes or revelation gifts

- Word of knowledge
- Word of wisdom
- Discerning of spirits

(3) Hands or power gifts

- Faith
- Healing
- Miracles

SESSION TWO — PROPHECY

training prophetic people to develop a strong clear prophetic flow

WORD OF KNOWLEDGE

Word of knowledge - Supernatural knowledge of the past or present that's revealed from God by the Holy Spirit. A word of knowledge is revealed more frequently to those that are called to be prophets or prophetess.

Jesus often prophesied using the word of knowledge

Example:
16 Jesus saith unto her, Go, call thy husband, and come hither.
17 The woman answered and said, I have no husband. Jesus said unto her, Thou hast well said, I have no husband:

Word of knowledge of the past & present

John 4:3-19 (KJV)
18 For thou hast had five husbands; and he whom thou now hast is not thy husband: in that saidst thou truly.
19 The woman saith unto him, Sir, I perceive that thou art a prophet.

John 4:28-29 (KJV)
28 The woman then left her waterpot, and went her way into the city, and saith to the men,
29 Come, see a man, which told me all things that ever I did: is not this the Christ?

Revelation knowledge defines God speaking to your mind the correct answer that is in the dictionary without opening a dictionary.

DECERNING OF SPIRITS

Once we're saved we receive the discerning of spirits with the Holy spirit.

Discerning which spirit is in operation
Hebrews 5:14 - to discern good & evil.

1.) It is the divine ability to see the present and activity of a spirit, that motivates a human being, whether good or bad. The revelation comes to the Body of Christ through the Holy Spirit.

2.) It gives the body of Christ insight into the spiritual realm.

What the discerning of spirits is not:

1.) The discerning of spirits is not anyway related to the nature.
2.) It's not through reading.
3.) Discerning of spirits has nothing to do with your soul, emotion, will, desire and intellect.
4.) It's not the gift of discernment, it's not the discerning of things but of spirits.
5.) It's not the discerning of demonic spirits.
6.) It's not a clash of human personalities.
7.) It's not the gift of superstition. Jezebel spirit is a controlling manipulating spirit.

SESSION TWO — PROPHECY

training prophetic people to develop a strong clear prophetic flow

REALMS OF PROPHECY

Prophecy is divine revelation from God given to a specific individual, that can be communicated in a prophetic mode, to a particular person, group, business, church, or individual, for edification, exhortation, comfort, and sometimes judgment and guidance.

WHAT IS A REALM?

1. A kingdom
2. Any field, sphere, or province [< regimen, system of government.]

3 REALMS OF PROPHECY

The Bible clearly states that there are different realms of prophetic flow, there are different administrations and operations of each of these realms. Therefore, it is important to know the difference in how each realm functions! The three realms to be discussed are.

• The Spirit of prophecy	— can come upon all believers
• The gift of prophecy	— resides inside the believer
• The office of the prophet	— God given mantle to function in

In defining this truth thru illustrations and teaching you will clearly see the difference in the functions of the three realms of prophecy. The first realm to be discussed is the Spirit of prophecy.

Note: The spirit of prophecy almost defines itself in the word itself, it's the spirit that one prophecies under. Meaning there's a spirit that a person, particularly a believer can come to encounter with that will encourage or impress one to speak out of the normal flow in an edifying, encouraging, exhorting, manner led by the Holy Spirit.

Therefore, God has raised up special people called patriarchs and prophets to be His spokesman to mankind.

> *Hebrews 1:1-3 (KJV)*
> *1 God, who at sundry times and in divers manners spake in time past unto the fathers by the prophets,*
> *2 Hath in these last days spoken unto us by his Son, whom he hath appointed heir of all things, by whom also he made the worlds;*
> *3 Who being the brightness of his glory, and the express image of his person, and upholding all things by the word of his power, when he had by himself purged our sins, sat down on the right hand of the Majesty on high;*

THE SOURCE OF REVELATION

Revelation from God is the nature of the prophetic utterance, whether inspirational or vocal. All revelation comes from a source.

Three sources of revelation

- The Holy Spirit - God
- The human spirit - Man
- The evil spirit - The Devil

MODES OF PROPHETIC REVELATION

Revelation that has been received from God, can be communicated in a prophetic mode, which is called prophecy. There are basically five different Hebrew and Aramaic words / roots from which all the old testament words for "prophecy" are derived. These two categories are firstly, words which emphasize the passive experience of receiving the prophetic message from God and secondly, words which emphasize the active experience of transmitting the prophetic message to the people. Which is called the communicative aspect of prophecy.
There's a human aspect and a divine aspect in prophecy.

SESSION TWO — PROPHECY

Ro'eh and Chozeh are both Hebrew words that describes seer.

Ro'eh "A seer. this Hebrew word occurs 21 times in the old testament. Essentially the root, ra'ah, means "to look at "or" to behold". This word is used of the prophet in his "seeing" or perceiving of God's message.

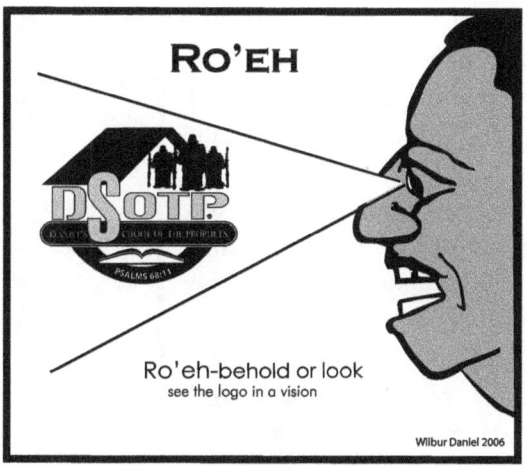

Ro'eh describes the prophetic revelation of the prophet through visions.

THE WORD SEER IS FOUND IN SCRIPTURE

1 Samuel 9:9-10 (KJV)

9 (Beforetime in Israel, when a man went to enquire of God, thus he spake, Come, and let us go to the seer: for he that is now called a prophet was beforetime called a Seer.)
10 Then said Saul to his servant, well said, come, let us go. So they went unto the city where the man of God was.

The receptive and communicative function

Chozeh - A seer. this Hebrew word occurs 16 times in the old testament. Also denotes the subjective experience of "seeing" God revealed message. Although these two terms may be used interchangeable. These two Hebrew terms, both meaning "seer" are synonyms for the word "prophet"
1 Samuel 9:9 show that the office of the prophet and seer are identical. The only difference in the words are in function,

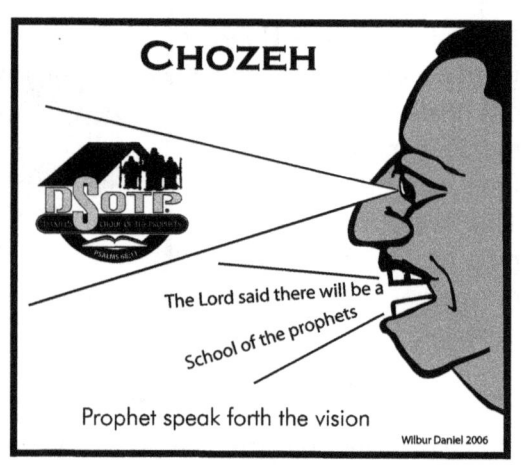

SEER

descriptive of the receptive function.

Passive experience of receiving the prophetic message from God.

PROPHET

descriptive of the communicative function.

Active experience of transmitting the prophetic message to the people.

The message from God may be communicated in different modes, styles, and ways.

SESSION TWO  PROPHECY

training prophetic people to develop a strong clear prophetic flow

A WORD FROM THE WORD

The creative utterance of God in Genesis chapter one sets the stage throughout Scripture for the Word of God to posses an intrinsic creative power! The Word of the Lord in prophecy is thus a dynamic, creative word.

The prophetic utterance is described in scripture as being the "word" (Heb., dabar) of the Lord. So Jeremiah in 1:9 records God's assurance to him of his prophetic call, "and the Lord said unto me, behold I have put my words (Heb., dabar) in thy mouth."

This Hebrew term for the word (dabar) carries with it the connotation of dynamic action. The basic etymological meaning of this term is "to be behind and drive forward" or "to drive forward that which is behind". Thus the "word" (dabar) is not only something spoken, but it "drives forward "to accomplish its message. The term developed somehow in Hebrew to portray the function of speaking.

The Hebrew language, especially verbs, have an inherent dynamic character. Hebrew verbs bear a basic meaning always expressing movement or activity, characteristic of the dynamic nature of Hebrew thinking.

When a Hebrew verb would express inaction such as a position of sitting or lying, it would be accomplished by a verb which also designates a movement or action. This is in direct contrast to Greek thinking and language which was by its nature static and without inherent movement.

This Hebrew term for "word" (dabar) meant not only a spoken word but also "deed". accomplishment was inherently an expected event as defined in the very meaning of the term. So Abraham's servant recounted to Isaac all the "things" (Heb., dabar,"words") he had done (Genesis 24:66. so likewise 1Kings 11: 41 mentions"...the rest of the act (Heb.,dabar) was identical with action. In Deuteronomy 18:22 the false prophet is proven to be false in that his words are counterfeit, empty words. They lack the inner power for accomplishing the content of the words: "When a prophet speaketh in the name of the Lord, if the thing follow not, nor come to pass, that is the which the Lord hath not spoken, but the prophet hath spoken it presumptuously: thou shalt not be afraid of him" Deuteronomy 18:22.

SESSION TWO — PROPHECY

The true prophet, on the other hand, speaks the Word of the Lord which "drives forward" to accomplish its own purpose. The "effective word" of prophecy is not alive and invested with a self-realizing power because of the "word" itself, but rather because it is characteristic of its source, Jehovah Himself. "word" (dabar) of the Lord is a manifestation of Jehovah and a revelation of essence. The living word that issued from God through the mouth of the prophets was never detached from God. This creative prophetic word is graphically illustrated in Ezekiel 37. As Ezekiel prophesies the dry bones, they become animate. Ezekiel's prophetic word has all the creative and life-giving power of God's Word, because his prophetic word is God's Word. The prophet's words possess mysterious or magical powers, but their dynamic nature is because these words are God's Word. The prophetic word which operates today in a presbytery through proven prophets is like God's words. Their prophetic utterances as the Words of God initiate a divine process to bring the prophetic message into effect in the lives of those so ministered over in a presbytery. The prophetic word that comes is a creative word.

This is further illustrated by Paul in his first epistle to Timothy. "Neglect not the gift that is in thee, which was given thee by prophecy, with the laying of the hands of the presbytery" (I Timothy 4:14). The gift that Timothy now possessed was given to him "by prophecy". This preposition in the Greek is dia, meaning literally "through", showing a channel. The prophetic-utterance the presbytery carried with it the creative power that "gave" (not only just informed) or channeled the gift from God to Timothy.

The gift was given to him through the prophetic utterance and subsequent, effectual work. This verse should also be joined with II Timothy 1:6, which show the gift also being imparted through the laying on of hands as well. However, a caution must be exercised concerning this truth.

Dabar

Decreeing

In order to decree, first an understanding of the word decree has to be defined.

(Several definitions relating to the word decree are listed below)
These most the interested definitions pertaining to Christian religion or spiritual terms.

1.) Official order: an order with the power of legislation issued by a ruler or other person or group with authority

2.) Divine will: in Christian belief, the will or purpose of God, interpreted through events considered to be God's doing

3.) An order usually having the force of law

4.) Religious ordinance enacted by council or titular head

28 Thou shalt also decree a thing, and it shall be established unto thee:
and the light shall shine upon thy ways.
Job 22:28 (KJV)

God has given us (Christians and believers) his written Word, the Bible. It's time to take the Word of God, search the scriptures, find what that council of God has legislated and authorized for us in heaven, and begin to degree, proclaim and declare that in our lives. Receive what our heavenly Father has already done in Christ. Begin to **decree, proclaim and declare** the things He has already completed at the Cross.

Declaring

State emphatically and authoritatively. Example to declare God's Word with authority. We should speak the Word in faith with authority believe that which we speak will come to past, because God's WORD is forever settled in Heaven and can't be changed.

KNOW YOUR SEASON

1 To every thing there is a season, and a time to every purpose under the heaven:
Eccl 3:1 (KJV)

Seasons can be referred to as chapters in your life. In each chapter or season there is a purpose for that season. Look for the fruit and purpose of the season or chapter you are in. Seasons can seem to be bad to you, but we know God doesn't make mistakes, there's a lesson or purpose for that season. Seek God through prayer and fasting and ask him what is the purpose for this season and Lord may the fruit of this season be blessed.

Romans 8:28 (KJV)

28 And we know that all things work together for good to them that love God, to them who are the called according to his purpose.

Let's face it, we've all walked through hopelessness and despair. But in the midst of these trials, God is completing us; He is finishing the good work He started. One thing I've not only learned yet witnessed with my very own eyes is that God does nothing without purpose. It is in the depths of despair that He has a plan and purpose - for us to trust, lean on and rely on Him and to remember that you're only passing through this desert - it is NOT a dwelling place. Selah!

GOD'S
PRE-WRITTEN BOOK FOR YOUR LIFE

God has given prophets the authority in the spirit realm to access the perfect law of liberty on the behalf of another individual life, plans purpose, and destiny. Prophets are able to look into the perfect law of liberty, and see God's pre-written course for man, and minister the mind of the Lord for that individual.

This revelation comes from God only, and is revealed to certain individuals that are mature in the Lord. God has refined these individuals by processing them over a period of time, imparting spiritual and natural knowledge, perfecting their skills and talents, allowing them to have a thorough revelation and understanding of His Word and the kingdom protocol. This process can and may take several years to develop depending on the realm, or level of ministry He assigns you to.

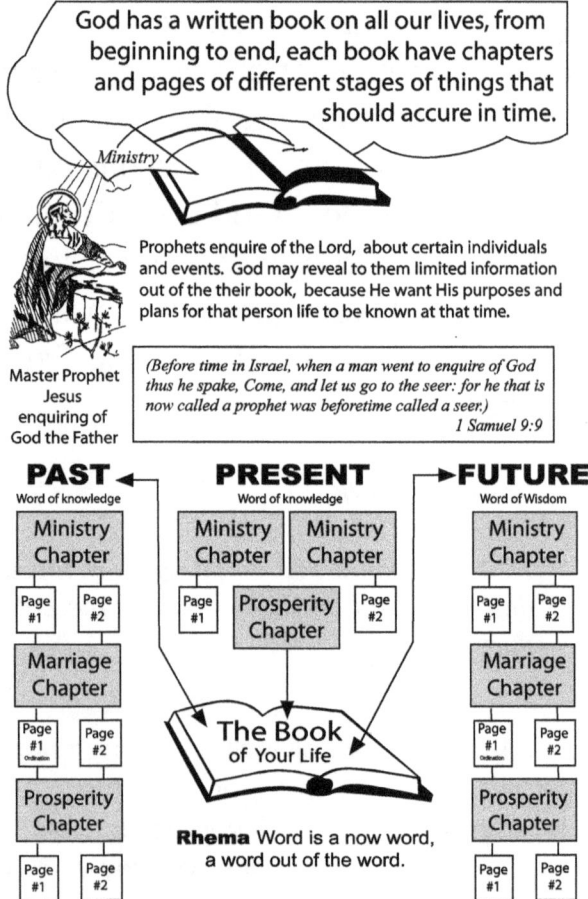

God has a written book on all our lives, from beginning to end, each book have chapters and pages of different stages of things that should accure in time.

Master Prophet Jesus enquiring of God the Father

Prophets enquire of the Lord, about certain individuals and events. God may reveal to them limited information out of the their book, because He want His purposes and plans for that person life to be known at that time.

(Before time in Israel, when a man went to enquire of God thus he spake, Come, and let us go to the seer: for he that is now called a prophet was beforetime called a seer.)
1 Samuel 9:9

PAST — Word of knowledge
PRESENT — Word of knowledge
FUTURE — Word of Wisdom

The Book of Your Life

Rhema Word is a now word, a word out of the word.

— Graphics by Wilbur Daniel

But whoso looketh into the perfect law of liberty, and continueth therein, he being not a forgetful hearer, but a doer of the work, this man shall be blessed in his deed.
James 1:25 (KJV)

REALMS OF PROPHECY

THE CREATIVE SPOKEN WORD

Two different examples of the creative spoken word.

1st Example:

> The creative spoken word of the prophet, is the prophet's creative spoken word, that the Lord honours and brings to pass.

1 Sam 3:19-20 (KJV)
19 And Samuel grew, and the LORD was with him, and did let none of his words fall to the ground.
20 And all Israel from Dan even to Beersheba knew that Samuel was established to be a prophet of the LORD.

2nd Example:

> The creative spoken word of the Lord, is to speak the heart, mind and message of the Lord prophetically, thus saith the Lord God

1 Then Elisha said, Hear ye the word of the LORD; Thus saith the LORD, Tomorrow about this time shall a measure of fine flour be sold for a shekel, and two measures of barley for a shekel, in the gate of Samaria.

SESSION TWO  PROPHECY

training prophetic people to develop a strong clear prophetic flow

THE CREATIVE SPOKEN WORD OF THE LORD

*is thus saith the LORD
that the prophet speak*

1 Kings 17:8-16 (KJV)

*8 And the word of the LORD came unto him, saying,
9 Arise, get thee to Zarephath, which belongeth to Zidon, and dwell there: behold, I have commanded a widow woman there to sustain thee.
10 So he arose and went to Zarephath. And when he came to the gate of the city, behold, the widow woman was there gathering of sticks: and he called to her, and said, Fetch me, I pray thee, a little water in a vessel, that I may drink.
11 And as she was going to fetch it, he called to her, and said, Bring me, I pray thee, a morsel of bread in thine hand.
12 And she said, As the LORD thy God liveth, I have not a cake, but an handful of meal in a barrel, and a little oil in a cruse: and, behold, I am gathering two sticks, that I may go in and dress it for me and my son, that we may eat it, and die.
13 And Elijah said unto her, Fear not; go and do as thou hast said: but make me thereof a little cake first, and bring it unto me, and after make for thee and for thy son.
14 For thus saith the LORD God of Israel, The barrel of meal shall not waste, neither shall the cruse of oil fail, until the day that the LORD sendeth rain upon the earth.
15 And she went and did according to the saying of Elijah: and she, and he, and her house, did eat many days.
16 And the barrel of meal wasted not, neither did the cruse of oil fail, according to the word of the LORD, which he spake by Elijah.*

THE CREATIVE SPOKEN WORD OF THE PROPHET/PROPHETESS

THE CREATIVE SPOKEN WORD
of the prophet/prophetess

2 Kings 4:1-7 (KJV)

1 Now there cried a certain woman of the wives of the sons of the prophets unto Elisha, saying, Thy servant my husband is dead; and thou knowest that thy servant did fear the LORD: and the creditor is come to take unto him my two sons to be bondmen.
2 And Elisha said unto her, What shall I do for thee? tell me, what hast thou in the house? And she said, Thine handmaid hath not any thing in the house, save a pot of oil.
3 Then he said, Go, borrow thee vessels abroad of all thy neighbours, even empty vessels; borrow not a few.
4 And when thou art come in, thou shalt shut the door upon thee and upon thy sons, and shalt pour out into all those vessels, and thou shalt set aside that which is full.
5 So she went from him, and shut the door upon her and upon her sons, who brought the vessels to her; and she poured out.
6 And it came to pass, when the vessels were full, that she said unto her son, Bring me yet a vessel. And he said unto her, There is not a vessel more. And the oil stayed.
7 Then she came and told the man of God. And he said, Go, sell the oil, and pay thy debt, and live thou and thy children of the rest.

SESSION TWO  PROPHECY

training prophetic people to develop a strong clear prophetic flow

THE CREATIVE SPOKEN WORD OF THE PROPHET

EXAMPLE OF CREATIVE SPOKEN WORD
to the prophet/prophetess

2 Kings 4:2-
A demand for the creative spoken word to be released

1 Now there cried a certain woman of the wives of the sons of the prophets unto Elisha, saying, Thy servant my husband is dead; and thou knowest that thy servant did fear the LORD: and the creditor is come to take unto him my two sons to be bondmen.
2 Kings 4:1 (KJV)

- What shall I do for thee?
- Tell me
- What hast thou in the house?

(Highlight) - In verse 2, 2 Kings 4:2

What shall I do for thee?
(I is referred to as Samuel) not thus saith the Lord!

8 - CREATIVE SPOKEN WORD
of the prophet/Elisha

2 Kings 4:3

SESSION TWO  **PROPHECY**

training prophetic people to develop a strong clear prophetic flow

THE CREATIVE SPOKEN WORD OF THE PROPHET

EXAMPLE OF CREATIVE SPOKEN WORD
to the prophet/prophetess

   2 Kings 4:2

8 - CREATIVE SPOKEN WORDS
of the prophet/Elisha

   2 Kings 4:3

1. Then he said go

2. Borrow vessels of thy neighbors

3. Borrow not a few

4. When thou art come in
   shut the door upon thou and thy sons

5. Pour out into all the vessels

6. And thou shalt set aside that which is full

7. Go, sell the oil

8. Live thou and thy children of the rest.

DREAMS

GOD IS THE INTERPRETER OF DREAMS

⁸ *And they said unto him, We have dreamed a dream, and there is no interpreter of it. And Joseph said unto them, Do not interpretations belong to God? tell me them, I pray you.*
  Gen 40:8 (KJV)

³² *And for that the dream was doubled unto Pharaoh twice; it is because the thing is established by God, and God will shortly bring it to pass.*
  Gen 41:32 (KJV)

Six Helpful Points for Remembering Dreams

Even though I remember a lot of my dreams, I tend to get hung up on the ones I don't remember. I'll sit up in my bed, trying my best to remember what I dreamed before it fades away. Sometimes I'm able to recall parts of the dream, but as much as I try, I just can't remember all of it. We dream about every hour and a half and the longest dreams last from thirty to forty-five minutes. One would think that so many dreams unfolding each time we sleep would leave a more lasting impression. So why don't they? They can if you're willing to do a little work. If you want to tap into your subconscious and start recalling your dreams, these points will help get you started.

1. Purchase Wilbur Daniel Prophetic Dream Journal

Writing our dreams down as soon as we wake is one of the best ways to remember them; it also helps us decipher them since we're able to reference them at any time. Wilbur Daniel suggestions for remembering our dreams, he recommends investing in a paperback dream journal that you can to enter at least one dream in it every night for an entire month. Once you've got your journal, on the left side write your dream. On the right side, give your interpretation of it.
When writing down your dreams, don't worry about grammar, punctuation, or the sequence of events. Concentrate on getting it all on paper as fast as you can before it fades away. When the month is up, look

back through your dreams. You'll be amazed at what you remembered and you'll have a lot more insight into what's influencing your dreams.

2. Identify Your Dreams With a Title

If you wake up and don't have time to journal, create a title for your dream and write that down instead. You should title dreams in your dream journal anyway, but this can be an effective way of remembering. Use the title of your dream as often as you can throughout the day, whether you're telling others about it or just trying to remember more details. When you have time to go back, expand on the title as much as you can. This could give you more clues into what you dreamed.

3. Draw Pictures Instead of Words As Often As Possible

If the idea of journaling all your dreams is intimidating, try drawing them. If you're better at images than words, this might be the best technique for you. Buy a Wilbur Daniel dream journal sketchbook and keep it by your bed with a pencil nearby. When you wake up, draw images you saw in your dreams. They don't have to be masterpieces of art, just stick figures or colors you remember. Once you get all the images down, go back and try to connect them to reconstruct your dream.

4. Wake Yourself Up

Try waking yourself up at different times of the night to remember more dreams. Set an alarm for early in the morning and when it goes off, challenge yourself to remember what you were dreaming.

    Tips: • Drink a glass of water before you go to bed.
            • Set the alarm clock for a specific time

5. Get Yourself in the Right Mind Set

Before going to bed, say aloud, "I will remember my dreams tonight." When you wake up, lay still in bed for a couple of minutes, eyes closed, and try to remember. Once you start remembering, sit still a little longer and try to reach for more. We all dream every night; we just don't always remember them. If we make a conscious decision to remember our dreams and try a few new techniques, we're bound to get a little closer to our own dream worlds.

OTHER THAN GOD KNOW THAT YOU'RE IN CONTROL

The only way God could stop the people of Babel, was to confuse their language. They were using what God gave them unity.

Gen 11:1-9

1 And the whole earth was of one language, and of one speech.
2 And it came to pass, as they journeyed from the east, that they found a plain in the land of Shinar; and they dwelt there.
3 And they said one to another, Go to, let us make brick, and burn them throughly. And they had brick for stone, and slime had they for morter.
4 And they said, Go to, let us build us a city and a tower, whose top may reach unto heaven; and let us make us a name, lest we be scattered abroad upon the face of the whole earth.
5 And the LORD came down to see the city and the tower, which the children of men builded.
6 And the LORD said, Behold, the people is one, and they have all one language; and this they begin to do: and now nothing will be restrained from them, which they have imagined to do.
7 Go to, let us go down, and there confound their language, that they may not understand one another's speech.
8 So the LORD scattered them abroad from thence upon the face of all the earth: and they left off to build the city.
9 Therefore is the name of it called Babel; because the LORD did there confound the language of all the earth: and from thence did the LORD scatter them abroad upon the face of all the earth.

INNER COUNCIL OF THE LORD

There's a road that travels around the world,
there's a path that leads to a destination,
there's a bridge that crosses over water,
there's a river that flows continually,
there's a plane that can fly in midair,
and there's the realm of the Spirit
where all mysteries, wisdom, knowledge,
understanding and the perfect will
of God is revealed.
That's where I want to be
—— Wilbur Daniel

INSIGHT, FORESIGHT, AND VISION

INSIGHT

Insight is when God allows or places you into a situation, location, place such as a job or ministry. Inside these places He allows you to see the inside circumstances such as decrimination, poverty, and other character and integrity issues. This allows you to know how to pray, if you wasn't inside these places with is insight you couldn't see it, therefore you wouldn't know how to pray over that situation.

FORESIGHT

Foresight is your calendar, dreams, word of wisdom, pending events, this allows you to look ahead and plan, use strategy, and wisdom.

Proverbs 22:3 A Prudent man foreseeth evil, and hideth himself; but the simple pass on and are punished.

VISION

Vision is the written plan of how you get to where God say you can go. *(Hab 2:1-4)*

Hab 2:1-4 (KJV)

1 I will stand upon my watch, and set me upon the tower, and will watch to see what he will say unto me, and what I shall answer when I am reproved.
2 And the LORD answered me, and said, Write the vision, and make it plain upon tables, that he may run that readeth it.
3 For the vision is yet for an appointed time, but at the end it shall speak, and not lie: though it tarry, wait for it; because it will surely come, it will not tarry.
4 Behold, his soul which is lifted up is not upright in him: but the just shall live by his faith.

training prophetic people to develop a strong clear prophetic flow

Session Three
PROPHETS

SESSION THREE  PROPHETS

training prophetic people to develop a strong clear prophetic flow

Different Kinds of
PROPHETS

Modern Day Prophets
Canonical Prophets
Northern Prophets
Southern Prophets
Scribal Prophets
Exile Prophets
Advent Prophets
Court Prophets
Major Prophets
Minor Prophets
False Prophets

Why Prophet's

God has chosen (elected) special men, named prophets (Nabi or Seers) to be a channel which he communicate through to man.

Prophet's Are GOD's communication channel

*The word **CHANNEL** is a*

3. A strait

4. A tubular passage

6. **CHANNELS** are official routes of communication

Prayer is essential to the prophet's life

Prayer is the way prophets communicate with God to get counsel from the Lord. God gives counsel to prophets for a certain geographical area and people, that they may live a quite and peaceful life in that area.

I Timothy 2:2

THE MODERN DAY PROPHET

> People look for prophets to be mystical, with a shining halo around their heads and long staffs in their hands. However, God has proven that prophets are real people just like you and me.

5 Which in other ages was not made known unto the sons of men, as it is now revealed unto his holy apostles and prophets by the Spirit;
 Eph 3:5 (KJV)

Each prophet's ministry was unique, because of his task or assignment from God, which varied by

- Message
- Symbolic Acts
- Lifestyle
- Time Period
- Culture

- Kings
- Principalities
- Spiritual Warfare
- Sins of the people
- Geographical Location

A MUST

> A prophet must pray
> to get the mind of God,
> for a prophet must flow
> in revelation knowledge.
>
> A prophet must have
> insight, foresight and vision
> along with wisdom and knowledge.

Isaiah 33:6
*6 And wisdom and knowledge
shall be the stability of thy times,
and strength of salvation:
the fear of the LORD is his treasure.*

> A prophet speaks only what
> God is saying no additives!

*1 Kings 22:14
And Micaiah said, As the LORD liveth,
what the LORD saith unto me, that will I speak.*

THE LORD ESTABLISHES THE PROPHET

1 Sam 3:19-20 (KJV)
19 And Samuel grew, and the LORD was with him, and did let none of his words fall to the ground.
20 And all Israel from Dan even to Beersheba knew that Samuel was established to be a prophet of the LORD.

2 Chron 20:20 (KJV)
20 And they rose early in the morning, and went forth into the wilderness of Tekoa: and as they went forth, Jehoshaphat stood and said, Hear me, O Judah, and ye inhabitants of Jerusalem; Believe in the LORD your God, so shall ye be established; believe his prophets, so shall ye prosper.

Job 22:28 (KJV)
28 Thou shalt also decree a thing, and it shall be established unto thee: and the light shall shine upon thy ways.

1 Peter 5:10 (KJV)
10 But the God of all grace, who hath called us unto his eternal glory by Christ Jesus, after that ye have suffered a while, make you perfect, stablish, strengthen, settle you.

THE LORD ESTABLISHES THE PROPHET

1 Sam 9:6-10 (KJV)
6 And he said unto him, Behold now, there is in this city a man of God, and he is an honourable man; all that he saith cometh surely to pass: now let us go thither; peradventure he can shew us our way that we should go.
7 Then said Saul to his servant, But, behold, if we go, what shall we bring the man? for the bread is spent in our vessels, and there is not a present to bring to the man of God: what have we?
8 And the servant answered Saul again, and said, Behold, I have here at hand the fourth part of a shekel of silver: that will I give to the man of God, to tell us our way.
9 (Beforetime in Israel, when a man went to enquire of God, thus he spake, Come, and let us go to the seer: for he that is now called a Prophet was beforetime called a Seer.)
10 Then said Saul to his servant, Well said; come, let us go. So they went unto the city where the man of God was.

SESSION THREE  PROPHETS

training prophetic people to develop a strong clear prophetic flow

EVERY PROPHET MUST BE TIME PROVEN

> After 80 years of training, Moses was
> time-proven as a prophet and
> commanded by God to go back to Egypt
> as the deliverer to lead God's people out of bondage.
> Moses life was divided
> into three 40 year periods.
> 40 years in Egypt
> 40 years in the desert
> time-proven at 80 years old
> and 40 years in the wilderness
> A total of 120 years.

I thought being a prophet was something that happens quick, but God's process takes you on a journey of a thousand miles, beginning with one step. Each step is carefully monitored by God, He makes sure you place each step precisely as He says.

- Each phase of your journey has a season that you will want to exhaust and fulfill everything that's in that season.

reference on page 130, 131

PROPHETS MUST BE BROKEN

> Moses was exhausted to the point he fell on his face, strengthless. Then God could move because Moses's strength was out of his way. Moses came to his wit's end on the back side of the desert. Man's extremity is God's opportunity.

Psalms 107:23-29

They that go down to the sea in ships, that do business in great waters; These see the works of the LORD, and his wonders in the deep. For he commandeth, and raiseth the stormy wind, which lifteth up the waves thereof. They mount up to the heaven, they go down again to the depths: their soul is melted because of trouble. They reel to and fro, and stagger like a drunken man, and are at their wits' end. Then they cry unto the LORD in their trouble, and he bringeth them out of their distresses. He maketh the storm a calm, so that the waves thereof are still.

OFFICE OF THE PROPHET

> The Lord said to me that the office of the prophet is a headship gift. The only way you can get into this position is that I allow you to.

Eph 4:8 (KJV)
8 Wherefore he saith, When he ascended up on high, he led captivity captive, and gave gifts unto men.

Eph 4:11 (KJV)
11 And he gave some, apostles; and some, prophets; and some, evangelists; and some, pastors and teachers;

John 15:16 (KJV)
16 Ye have not chosen me, but I have chosen you, and ordained you, that ye should go and bring forth fruit, and that your fruit should remain: that whatsoever ye shall ask of the Father in my name, he may give it you.

SESSION THREE — PROPHETS

October 19, 2009

──── THE OFFICE ────

Thus saith the Lord God, to have 100% legal authority naturally and spiritually, one must be set apart and consecrated into one of the fivefold headship government offices in the body of Christ.

1. Apostle 3. Evangelist 5. Teacher
2. Prophet 4. Pastor

Now I have brought you _____ unto me, How? Through tutors, governors, fathers, teachers and pastors. using them to train and teach you my ways and my word. Now that you are mature spiritually, and know me, I have need of you in the kingdom. *Galatians 4:1-4*

The _____ office is one of the five highest spiritual offices and authority in the body of Christ. No one can come into a office of himself, God said thru your obedience to him, he sets your course in life that you should follow that will lead to consecration and separation unto Him. Now that God has established you in a spiritual position of authority in the Kingdom. He can use you however He pleases to advance the Kingdom of God on earth. Knowing this be encouraged for it is His good pleasure to bless you, and use you for the kingdom, even as He used our forefathers.

- *Abraham* • *Moses* • *Samuel* • *Elijah*

BE ENCOURAGED YOU ARE IN MY CARE NOW!

SESSION THREE  PROPHETS

IN GOD'S CARE

1 Chron 21:1-13

1 And Satan stood up against Israel, and provoked David to number Israel.
2 And David said to Joab and to the rulers of the people, Go, number Israel from Beersheba even to Dan; and bring the number of them to me, that I may know it.
7 And God was displeased with this thing; therefore he smote Israel.
8 And David said unto God, I have sinned greatly, because I have done this thing: but now, I beseech thee, do away the iniquity of thy servant; for I have done very foolishly.
9 And the LORD spake unto Gad, David's seer, saying,
10 Go and tell David, saying, Thus saith the LORD, I offer thee three things: choose thee one of them, that I may do it unto thee.
11 So Gad came to David, and said unto him, Thus saith the LORD, Choose thee
12 Either three years' famine; or three months to be destroyed before thy foes, while that the sword of thine enemies overtaketh thee; or else three days the sword of the LORD, even the pestilence, in the land, and the angel of the LORD destroying throughout all the coasts of Israel. Now therefore advise thyself what word I shall bring again to him that sent me.

13 And David said unto Gad, I am in a great strait: let me fall now into the hand of the LORD; for very great are his mercies: but let me not fall into the hand of man.

| SESSION THREE |  | PROHETS |

GOD BROUGHT YOU OUT

Ex 19:4 (KJV)

4 Ye have seen what I did unto the Egyptians, and how I bare you on eagles' wings, and brought you unto myself.

God has meet needs by way of allowing you to be reconnected with a distant relative and in a short period of time things for you change drastically. Out of 20 or more enquiries, this relative is the only open door of opportunity.

Look back over your life and recall many incidents where your found yourself in God's care.

Psalms 27:10 (KJV)

10 When my father and my mother forsake me, then the LORD will take me up.

SESSION THREE  PROPHETS

training prophetic people to develop a strong clear prophetic flow

MINISTRY

The word ministry always refer to a service to the people. Ministries is the avenue or channel God uses through you to be of service to the people on the behalf of Christ. God has given each fivefold or government office a ministry, meaning fivefold offices have a unique grace and measure of anointing to fulfill their spiritual service to the people, this is called ministry. The service they provide can be spiritual or combined with natural skills and talents that God has ordained to be a tool to accommodate them in their individual ministry.

Paul and Barnabas are chosen for ministry to the Gentiles

Acts 13:1-5 (KJV)
1 Now there were in the church that was at Antioch certain prophets and teachers; as Barnabas, and Simeon that was called Niger, and Lucius of Cyrene, and Manaen, which had been brought up with Herod the tetrarch, and Saul.
2 As they ministered to the Lord, and fasted, the Holy Ghost said, Separate me Barnabas and Saul for the work whereunto I have called them.
3 And when they had fasted and prayed, and laid their hands on them, they sent them away.
4 So they, being sent forth by the Holy Ghost, departed unto Seleucia; and from thence they sailed to Cyprus. 5 And when they were at Salamis, they preached the word of God in the synagogues of the Jews:

MINISTRY OF THE PROPHET

10 I have also spoken unto the prophets, and I have multiplied visions; and by the ministry of the prophets have I used similitudes.
Hosea 12:10 (ASV)

The ministry of the Prophet is calling and anointing in the stage and development that God has given you in your spiritual and natural skills, talents, anointing, to translate into ministry (or service) for the people, saints and sinners.
- Saint - It's for the building up and edifying, according to Ephesians 4:12
- Sinner - For the sinner it's the measure of grace and anointing through Spiritual and natural resources that God has given you to win over the sinner to Jesus Christ.

Eph 4:1-13 (ASV)
*1 I therefore, the prisoner in the Lord, beseech you to **walk worthily of the calling wherewith ye were called,***
2 with all lowliness and meekness, with longsuffering, forbearing one another in love;
3 giving diligence to keep the unity of the Spirit in the bond of peace.
4 There is one body, and one Spirit, even as also ye were called in one hope of your calling;
5 one Lord, one faith, one baptism,
6 one God and Father of all, who is over all, and through all, and in all.
7 But unto each one of us was the grace given according to the measure of the gift of Christ.
8 Wherefore he saith, When he ascended on high, he led captivity captive, And gave gifts unto men.
9 (Now this, He ascended, what is it but that he also descended into the lower parts of the earth?
10 He that descended is the same also that ascended far above all the heavens, that he might fill all things.)
11 And he gave some to be apostles; and some, prophets; and some, evangelists; and some, pastors and teachers;
12 for the perfecting of the saints, unto the work of ministering, unto the building up of the body of Christ:
13 till we all attain unto the unity of the faith, and of the knowledge of the Son of God, unto a fullgrown man, unto the measure of the stature of the fulness of Christ:

MINISTRY OF THE PROPHET

Each prophet's ministry were unique because of his task or assignment from God, which varied by;

- Message
- Symbolic acts
- Lifestyle
- Time period
- Culture

- Kings
- Principalities
- Spiritual warfare
- Sins of the people
- Geographical Location

Hosea 12:10 (KJV)

10 I have also spoken by the prophets, and I have multiplied visions, and used similitudes, by the ministry of the prophets.

SESSION THREE PROPHETS

training prophetic people to develop a strong clear prophetic flow

THE PROPHET'S MESSAGE

1:1-6 (KJV)

1 *In the eighth month, in the second year of Darius, came the word of the LORD unto Zechariah, the son of Berechiah, the son of Iddo the prophet, saying,*
2 *The LORD hath been sore displeased with your fathers.*
3 *Therefore say thou unto them, Thus saith the LORD of hosts; Turn ye unto me, saith the LORD of hosts, and I will turn unto you, saith the LORD of hosts.*
4 *Be ye not as your fathers, unto whom the former prophets have cried, saying, Thus saith the LORD of hosts; Turn ye now from your evil ways, and from your evil doings: but they did not hear, nor hearken unto me, saith the LORD.*
5 *Your fathers, where are they? and the prophets, do they live for ever?*
6 *But my words and my statutes, which I commanded my servants the prophets, did they not take hold of your fathers? and they returned and said, Like as the LORD of hosts thought to do unto us, according to our ways, and according to our doings, so hath he dealt with us. Zech*

PROPHETS PREPARED THE WAY FOR THE COMING OF THE LORD

> Prophets like John the Baptist, and Malachi made straight paths for the coming of the Lord Jesus Christ

Mal 3:1 (KJV)
1 Behold, I will send my messenger, and he shall prepare the way before me: and the Lord, whom ye seek, shall suddenly come to his temple, even the messenger of the covenant, whom ye delight in: behold, he shall come, saith the LORD of hosts.

Matt 3:1-6 (KJV)
1 In those days came John the Baptist, preaching in the wilderness of Judaea,
2 And saying, Repent ye: for the kingdom of heaven is at hand.
3 For this is he that was spoken of by the prophet Esaias, saying, The voice of one crying in the wilderness, Prepare ye the way of the Lord, make his paths straight.
4 And the same John had his raiment of camel's hair, and a leathern girdle about his loins; and his meat was locusts and wild honey.
5 Then went out to him Jerusalem, and all Judaea, and all the region round about Jordan,
6 And were baptized of him in Jordan, confessing their sins

The D's

- They came that were in distress.

- They came that were in debt.

- They came that were discontented.

Notice: When you are in the D's God will hide you. Most of the time it's not the rich that come seeking Christ and the prophet, it's those that are in the D's from above.

David in the cave of Adullam, being chased by Saul stayed until the appointed time. *1 Sam. 22:1-2*

Scripture states Jesus came forth at the appointed time. *Galatians 4:4*

1 Sam 22:1-2 (KJV)

David therefore departed thence, and escaped to the cave Adullam: and when his brethren and all his father's house heard it, they went down thither to him. And every one that was in distress, and every one that was in debt, and every one that was discontented, gathered themselves unto him; and he became a captain over them: and there were with him about four hundred men.

5 Major Prophets

(1) Isaiah
(2) Lamentation
(3) Daniel
(4) Jeremiah
(5) Ezekiel

12 Minor Prophets

(1) Hosea   (7) Nahum
(2) Joel   (8) Habakkuk
(3) Amos   (9) Zephaniah
(4) Obadiah   (10) Haggai
(5) Jonah   (11) Zechariah
(6) Micah   (12) Malachi

12 MINOR PROPHETS

Called the book of the Twelve Prophets

Collectively the minor prophets work to present one message reaffirming God's love and plans for His people Israel beyond His judgment on their sin.

—— 12 Minor Prophets ——

1. **Hosea:** God's love is constant and stubborn. It would not give up despite Israel's apostasy.

2. **Joel:** Sin is great and serious; judgment had to come.

3. **Amos:** Israel's sin and that of their neighbors was full; judgment.

4. **Obadiah:** God's rule is shown by judgment on Edom.

5. **Jonah:** God cared about Nineveh too.

6. **Micah** 4-5 (in the center of the whole): God's house (the Jerusalem temple) would be raised above all the mountains. All peoples could come to it for worship. Justice and mercy are more important than sacrifice.

7. **Nahum:** God's wrath was revealed in the destruction of Nineveh.

8. **Habakkuk:** The trials of faith in crisis because of Babylon had to be patiently endured.

9. **Zephaniah:** Joel's theme about the Day of the Lord was resumed.

10. **Haggai** and Zechariah 1-8: Zerubabbel's and Joshua's building the temple showed that the time for fulfillment of God's benevolent purposes for Jerusalem was near. It was happening.

11. **Zechariah** 9-14: The history of pre exilic Israel is summarized from viewpoint of post exilic Judaism under Persia's rule.

12. **Malachi:** God's love has been revealed.

training prophetic people to develop a strong clear prophetic flow

KNOWING YOUR OWN COMPANY

Paul in the New Testament had to go to his own company, like faith people, kindred spirit, prophetic people. Samuel traveled with the company of prophets. So what company are you keeping?   Acts 15:22, 32

1 Sam 19:20-24 (KJV)
And Saul sent messengers to take David: and when they saw the company of the prophets prophesying, and Samuel standing as appointed over them, the Spirit of God was upon the messengers of Saul, and they also prophesied. And when it was told Saul, he sent other messengers, and they prophesied likewise. And Saul sent messengers again the third time, and they prophesied also. Then went he also to Ramah, and came to a great well that is in Sechu: and he asked and said, Where are Samuel and David? And one said, Behold, they be at Naioth in Ramah. And he went thither to Naioth in Ramah: and the Spirit of God was upon him also, and he went on, and prophesied, until he came to Naioth in Ramah. And he stripped off his clothes also, and prophesied before Samuel in like manner, and lay down naked all that day and all that night. Wherefore they say, Is Saul also among the prophets?

SESSION THREE — PROPHETS

Samuel traveled in a circuit with a company of prophets. He also trained young prophets. Young prophets in the old testament trained at a school of the prophets headed by Samuel. This was a place where they socialized, had fellowship, did chores, studied the scripture, and learned how to hear the voice of God clearly. These prophets had a lot in common, they understood rejection, spiritual warfare and other things that occurred during the growth of a young prophet. Be careful and very aware that you are not in the company of people that don't understand or know how to comprehend who you are, because where you are not celebrated you are merely tolerated.

1 Sam 7:15-17 (KJV)
15 And Samuel judged Israel all the days of his life. 16 And he went from year to year in circuit to Bethel, and Gilgal, and Mizpeh, and judged Israel in all those places. 17 And his return was to Ramah; for there was his house; and there he judged Israel; and there he built an altar unto the LORD.

1 Sam 10:4-8 (KJV)
And they will salute thee, and give thee two loaves of bread; which thou shalt receive of their hands. 5 After that thou shalt come to the hill of God, where is the garrison of the Philistines: and it shall come to pass, when thou art come thither to the city, that thou shalt meet a company of prophets coming down from the high place with a psaltery, and a tabret, and a pipe, and a harp, before them; and they shall prophesy: 6 And the Spirit of the LORD will come upon thee, and thou shalt prophesy with them, and shalt be turned into another man. 7 And let it be, when these signs are come unto thee, that thou do as occasion serve thee; for God is with thee. 8 And thou shalt go down before me to Gilgal; and, behold, I will come down unto thee, to offer burnt offerings, and to sacrifice sacrifices of peace offerings: seven days shalt thou tarry, till I come to thee, and shew thee what thou shalt do.

THE SEED GROUP

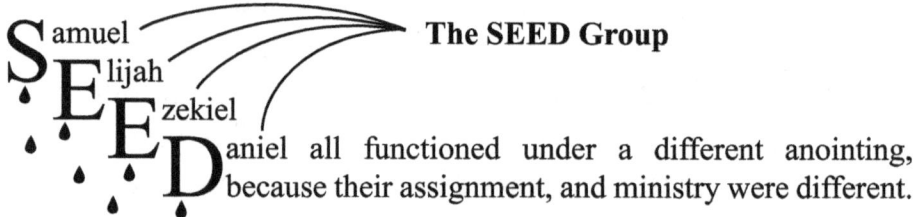

Samuel
Elijah
Ezekiel
Daniel all functioned under a different anointing, because their assignment, and ministry were different.

The SEED Group

This ability or anointing can be linked or associated with a Hebrew word called *chiro* - which means the supernatural empowerment of God to do special miracles, signs, wonders, as well as increased intelligence, unusual wisdom and uncanny logic.

The *chiros* anointing has been truly mistsaken with *charisma* - Christ's redemptive charisma, the new Creation Spirit given to those born again from God's spirit. Natural gifting, talents, and skills are also taken for the anointing. The Bible says gifts and calling come without repentance.

Gifts and talents say the minister is capable naturally for the work he or she has been called to; the anointing makes the minister divinely able. The chiro anointing is an upgrade or added divine power on natural talents, gifts, and skills, that comes from being baptized by the Holy Spirit, that God gives for a particular ministry call to powerfully effect His Body.

Once again this raises the question, why prophets?

God wants to communicate. He desires intimate fellowship with man rather than a distant relationship with humanity, but humanity is too busy to stop and receive the way He wants to communicate. Therefore God has chosen special people called prophets to be his communication channel.

1 Samuel 9:1-8

¹ Now there was a man of Benjamin, whose name *was* Kish, the son of Abiel, the son of Zeror, the son of Bechorath, the son of Aphiah, a Benjamite, a mighty man of power.

² And he had a son, whose name *was* Saul, a choice young man, and a goodly: and *there was* not among the children of Israel a goodlier person than he: from his shoulders and upward *he was* higher than any of the people.

³ And the asses of Kish Saul's father were lost. And Kish said to Saul his son, Take now one of the servants with thee, and arise, go seek the asses.

⁴ And he passed through mount Ephraim, and passed through the land of Shalisha, but they found *them* not: then they passed through the land of Shalim, and *there they were* not: and he passed through the land of the Benjamites, but they found *them* not.

⁵ *And* when they were come to the land of Zuph, Saul said to his servant that *was* with him, Come, and let us return; lest my father leave *caring* for the asses, and take thought for us.

⁶ And he said unto him, Behold now, *there is* in this city a man of God, and *he is* an honourable man; all that he saith cometh surely to pass: now let us go thither; peradventure he can shew us our way that we should go.

⁷ Then said Saul to his servant, But, behold, *if* we go, what shall we bring the man? for the bread is spent in our vessels, and *there is* not a present to bring to the man of God: what have we?

⁸ And the servant answered Saul again, and said, Behold, I have here at hand the fourth part of a shekel of silver: *that* will I give to the man of God, to tell us our way.

SAMUEL

Before I formed thee in the belly I knew thee; and before thou camest forth out of the womb I sanctified thee, and I ordained thee a prophet unto the nations.   Jeremiah: 1:5

The calling of Samuel

1 Sam 3:1-21 (KJV)

1 And the child Samuel ministered unto the LORD before Eli. And the word of the LORD was precious in those days; there was no open vision.
2 And it came to pass at that time, when Eli was laid down in his place, and his eyes began to wax dim, that he could not see;
3 And ere the lamp of God went out in the temple of the LORD, where the ark of God was, and Samuel was laid down to sleep;
4 That the LORD called Samuel: and he answered, Here am I.
5 And he ran unto Eli, and said, Here am I; for thou calledst me. And he said, I called not; lie down again. And he went and lay down.
6 And the LORD called yet again, Samuel. And Samuel arose and went to Eli, and said, Here am I; for thou didst call me. And he answered, I called not, my son; lie down again.
7 Now Samuel did not yet know the LORD, neither was the word of the LORD yet revealed unto him.
8 And the LORD called Samuel again the third time. And he arose and went to Eli, and said, Here am I; for thou didst call me. And Eli perceived that the LORD had called the child.
9 Therefore Eli said unto Samuel, Go, lie down: and it shall be, if he call thee, that thou shalt say, Speak, LORD; for thy servant heareth. So Samuel went and lay down in his place.
10 And the LORD came, and stood, and called as at other times, Samuel, Samuel. Then Samuel answered, Speak; for thy servant heareth.
11 And the LORD said to

Samuel, Behold, I will do a thing in Israel, at which both the ears of every one that heareth it shall tingle.
12 In that day I will perform against Eli all things which I have spoken concerning his house: when I begin, I will also make an end.
13 For I have told him that I will judge his house for ever for the iniquity which he knoweth; because his sons made themselves vile, and he restrained them not.
14 And therefore I have sworn unto the house of Eli, that the iniquity of Eli's house shall not be purged with sacrifice nor offering for ever.
15 And Samuel lay until the morning, and opened the doors of the house of the LORD. And Samuel feared to shew Eli the vision.
16 Then Eli called Samuel, and said, Samuel, my son. And he answered, Here am I.
17 And he said, What is the thing that the LORD hath said unto thee? I pray thee hide it not from me: God do so to thee, and more also, if thou hide any thing from me of all the things that he said unto thee.
18 And Samuel told him every whit, and hid nothing from him. And he said, It is the LORD: let him do what seemeth him good.
Samuel grows in favor
19 And Samuel grew, and the LORD was with him, and did let none of his words fall to the ground.
20 And all Israel from Dan even to Beersheba knew that Samuel was established to be a prophet of the LORD.
21 And the LORD appeared again in Shiloh: for the LORD revealed himself to Samuel in Shiloh by the word of the LORD.
1 Sam 3:1-21 (KJV)

1 Samuel 10: 1-16

Samuel anoints Saul

1 Then Samuel took a vial of oil, and poured *it* upon his head, and kissed him, and said, *Is it* not because the LORD hath anointed thee *to be* captain over his inheritance?

2 When thou art departed from me to day, then thou shalt find two men by Rachel's sepulchre in the border of Benjamin at Zelzah; and they will say unto thee, The asses which thou wentest to seek are found: and, lo, thy father hath left the care of the asses, and sorroweth for you, saying, What shall I do for my son?

3 Then shalt thou go on forward from thence, and thou shalt come to the plain of Tabor, and there shall meet thee three men going up to God to Bethel, one carrying three kids, and another carrying three loaves of bread, and another carrying a bottle of wine:

4 And they will salute thee, and give thee two *loaves* of bread; which thou shalt receive of their hands.

5 After that thou shalt come to the hill of God, where *is* the garrison of the Philistines: and it shall come to pass, when thou art come thither to the city, that thou shalt meet a company of prophets coming down from the high place with a psaltery, and a tabret, and a pipe, and a harp, before them; and they shall prophesy:

6 And the Spirit of the LORD will come upon thee, and thou shalt prophesy with them, and shalt be turned into another man.

7 And let it be, when these signs are come unto thee, *that* thou do as occasion serve thee; for God *is* with thee.

8 And thou shalt go down before me to Gilgal; and, behold, I will come down unto thee, to offer burnt offerings, *and* to sacrifice sacrifices of peace offerings: seven days shalt thou tarry, till I come to thee, and shew thee what thou shalt do.

Saul's heart is changed, and he prophesies

9 And it was *so*, that when he had turned his back to go from Samuel, God gave him another heart: and all those signs came to pass that day.

10 And when they came thither to the hill, behold, a company of prophets met him; and the Spirit of God came upon him, and he prophesied among them.

11 And it came to pass, when all that knew him beforetime saw that, behold, he prophesied among the prophets, then the people said one to another, What *is* this *that* is come unto the son of Kish? *Is* Saul also among the prophets?

12 And one of the same place answered and said, But who *is* their father? Therefore it became a proverb, *Is* Saul also among the prophets?

13 And when he had made an end of prophesying, he came to the high place.

14 And Saul's uncle said unto him and to his servant, Whither went ye? And he said, To seek the asses: and when we saw that *they were* no where, we came to Samuel.

15 And Saul's uncle said, Tell me, I pray thee, what Samuel said unto you.

16 And Saul said unto his uncle, He told us plainly that the asses were found. But of the matter of the kingdom, where of Samuel spake, he told him not.

1 Sam 10:1-16 (KJV)

Samuel Anoints Saul

Elijah

1 And Elijah the Tishbite, who was of the inhabitants of Gilead, said unto Ahab, As the LORD God of Israel liveth, before whom I stand, there shall not be dew nor rain these years, but according to my word.
1 Kings 17:1 (KJV)

Elijah Was A Tishbite
Eli'jah (my God is Jehovah) has been well entitled "the grandest and the most romantic character that Israel ever produced." "Elijah the Tishbite, . . . of the inhabitants of Gilead" is literally all that is given us to know of his parentage and locality. Of his appearance as he "stood before" Ahab (b.c. 910) with the suddenness of motion to this day characteristic of the Bedouins from his native hills, we can perhaps realize something from the touches, few but strong, of the narrative. His chief characteristic was his hair, long and thick, and hanging down his back. His ordinary clothing consisted of a girdle of skin round his loins, which he tightened when about to move quickly. 1 Kin 18:46 But in addition to this he occasionally wore the "mantle" or cape of sheepskin which has supplied us with one of our most familiar figures of speech. His introduction, in what we may call the first act of his life, is the most startling description. He suddenly appears before Ahab, prophesies a three-year drought in Israel, and proclaims the vengeance of Jehovah for the apostasy of the king. Obliged to flee from the vengeance of the king, or more probably the queen (comp. 1 Kin 19:2 he was directed to the brook Cherith. There in the hollow of the torrent bed he remained, supported in the miraculous manner with which we are all familiar, till the failing of the brook obliged him to forsake it. His next refuge was at Zarephath. Here in the house of the widow woman Elijah performed the miracles of prolonging the oil and the meal, and restored the son of the widow to life after his apparent death. 1 Kin 17. In this or some other retreat an interval of more than two years must have elapsed. The drought continued, and at last the full horrors of famine, caused by the failure of the crops, descended on Samaria. Again Elijah suddenly appears before Ahab. There are few more sublime stories in history than the account of the succeeding events—with the servant of Jehovah and his single attendant on the one hand, and the 850 prophets of Baal on the other; the altars, the descending fire of Jehovah consuming both sacrifice and altar; the rising storm, and the ride across the plain to Jezreel. 1 Kin 18. Jezebel vows vengeance, and again Elijah takes refuge in

SESSION THREE  PROPHETS

training prophetic people to develop a strong clear prophetic flow

---

flight into the wilderness, where he is again miraculously fed, and goes forward, in the strength of that food, a journey of forty days to the mount of God, even to Horeb, where he takes refuge in a cave, and witnesses a remarkable vision of Jehovah. 1 Kin 19:9-18 He receives the divine communication, and sets forth in search of Elisha, whom he finds ploughing in the field, and anoints him prophet in his place. ch. 19. For a time little is heard of Elijah, and Ahab and Jezebel probably believed they had seen the last of him. But after the murder of Naboth, Elijah, who had received an intimation from Jehovah of what was taking place, again suddenly appears before the king, and then follow Elijah's fearful denunciation of Ahab and Jezebel, which may possibly be recovered by putting together the words recalled by Jehu, 2 Kin 9:26, 36, 37 and those given in 1 Kin 21:19-25 A space of three or four years now elapses (comp. 1 Kin 22: 1, 51; 2 Kin 1:17 before we again catch a glimpse of Elijah. Ahaziah is on his death-bed, 1 Kin 22:51; 2 Kin 1:1, 2 and sends to an oracle or shrine of Baal to ascertain the issue of his illness; but Elijah suddenly appears on the path of the messengers, without preface or inquiry utters his message of death, and as rapidly disappears. The wrathful king sends two bands of soldiers to seize Elijah, and they are consumed with fire; but finally the prophet goes down and delivers to Ahaziah's face the message of death. Not long after, Elijah sent a message to Jehoram denouncing his evil doings, and predicting his death. 2 Chr 21:12-15 It was at Gilgal—probably on the western edge of the hills of Ephraim—that the prophet received the divine intimation that his departure was at hand. He was at the time with Elisha, who seems now to have become his constant companion, and who would not consent to leave him. "And it came to pass as they still went on and talked, that, behold, a chariot of fire and horses of fire, and parted them both asunder; and Elijah went up by a whirlwind into heaven." (b.c. 896.) Fifty men of the sons of the prophets ascended the abrupt heights behind the town, and witnessed the scene. How deep was the impression which he made on the mind of the nation may be judged of from the fixed belief which many centuries after prevailed that Elijah would again appear for the relief and restoration of his country, as Malachi prophesied. Mala 4:5 He spoke, but left no written words, save the letter to Jehoram king of Judah. 2 Chr 21:12-15
—Smith's Bible Dictionary

Elisha

Elisha Eli'sha (God his salvation), son of Shaphat of Abel-meholah; the attendant and disciple of Elijan, and subsequently his successor as prophet of the kingdom of Israel. The earliest mention of his name is in the command to Elijah in the cave at Horeb. 1 Kin 19:16, 17 (b.c. about 900.) Elijah sets forth to obey the command, and comes upon his successor engaged in ploughing. He crosses to him and throws over his shoulders the rough mantle—a token at once of investiture with the prophet's office and of adoption as a son. Elisha delayed merely to give the farewell kiss to his father and mother and preside at a parting feast with his people, and then followed the great prophet on his northward road. We hear nothing more of Elisha for eight years, until the translation of his master, when he reappears, to become the most prominent figure in the history of his country during the rest of his long life.

In almost every respect Elisha presents the most complete contrast to Elijah. Elijah was a true Bedouin child of the desert. If he enters a city it is only to deliver his message of fire and be gone. Elisha, on the other hand, is a civilized man, an inhabitant of cities. His dress was the ordinary garment of an Israelite, the beged, probably similar in form to the long abbeyeh of the modern Syrians. 2 Kin 2:12 His hair was worn trimmed behind, in contrast to the disordered locks of Elijah, and he used a walking-staff, 2 Kin 4:29 of the kind ordinarily carried by grave or aged citizens. Zech 8:4 After the departure of his master, Elisha returned to dwell at Jericho, 2 Kin 2:18 where he miraculously purified the springs. We next meet with Elisha at Bethel, in the heart of the country, on his way from Jericho to Mount Carmel. 2 Kin 2:23 The mocking children, Elisha's curse and the catastrophe which followed are familiar to all. Later he extricates Jehoram king of Israel, and the kings of Judah and Edom, from their difficulty in the campaign against Moab arising from want of water. 2 Kin 3:4-27 Then he multiplies the widow's oil. 2 Kin 4: 5 The next occurrence is at Shunem, where he is hospitably entertained by a woman of substance, whose son dies, and is brought to life again by Elisha. 2 Kin 4:8-37 Then at Gilgal he purifies the deadly pottage, 2 Kin 4:38-41 and multiplies the loaves. 2 Kin 4: 42-44 The simple records of these domestic incidents amongst the sons of the prophets are now interrupted by an occurrence of a more important character. 2 Kin 5:1-27 The chief captain of the army of Syria, Naaman, is attacked with leprosy, and is sent by an Israelite maid to the prophet Elisha, who directs him to dip seven times in the Jordan, which he does and is healed, 2 Kin 5:1-14 while Naaman's servant, Gehazi, he strikes with leprosy for his unfaithfulness. 2 Kin 5:20-27 Again the scene changes. It is probably at Jericho that Elisha causes the iron axe to swim. 2 Kin 6:1-7 A band of Syrian marauders are sent to seize him, but are struck blind, and he misleads them to Samaria, where they find themselves in the presence of the Israelite king and his troops. 2 Kin 6:8-23 During the famine in Samaria, 2 Kin 6:24-33 he prophesied incredible plenty, 2 Kin 7:1-2 which was soon fulfilled. 2 Kin 7:3-20 We next find the prophet at Damascus. Benhadad the king is sick, and sends to Elisha by Hazael to know the result. Elisha prophesies the king's death, and announces to Hazael that he is to succeed to the throne. 2 Kin 8:7, 15 Finally this prophet of God, after having filled the position for sixty years, is found on his death-bed in his own house. 2 Kin 13:14-19 The power of the prophet, however, does not terminate with his death. Even in the tomb he restores the dead to life. 2 Kin 13:21

—Smith's Bible Dictionary

DANIEL

DANIEL HAD AN EXCELLENT SPIRIT

Dan 6:3 (KJV)
3 Then this Daniel was preferred above the presidents and princes, because an excellent spirit was in him; and the king thought to set him over the whole realm.

Dan 5:12-14 (KJV)
12 Forasmuch as an excellent spirit, and knowledge, and understanding, interpreting of dreams, and shewing of hard sentences, and dissolving of doubts, were found in the same Daniel, whom the king named Belteshazzar: now let Daniel be called, and he will shew the interpretation. 13 Then was Daniel brought in before the king. And the king spake and said unto Daniel, Art thou that Daniel, which art of the children of the captivity of Judah, whom the king my father brought out of Jewry? 14 I have even heard of thee, that the spirit of the gods is in thee, and that light and understanding and excellent wisdom is found in thee.

1 In the third year of the reign of Jehoiakim king of Judah came Nebuchadnezzar king of Babylon unto Jerusalem, and besieged it.
2 And the Lord gave Jehoiakim king of Judah into his hand, with part of the vessels of the house of God: which he carried into the land of Shinar to the house of his god; and he brought the vessels into the treasure house of his god.
3 And the king spake unto Ashpenaz the master of his eunuchs, that he should bring certain of the children of Israel, and of the king's seed, and of the princes;
4 Children in whom was no blemish, but well favoured, and skilful in all wisdom, and cunning in knowledge, and understanding science, and such as had ability in them to stand in the king's palace, and whom they might teach the learning and the tongue of the Chaldeans.
5 And the king appointed them a daily provision of the king's meat, and of the wine which he drank: so nourishing them three years, that at the end thereof they might stand before the king.
6 Now among these were of the children of Judah, Daniel, Hananiah, Mishael, and Azariah:
7 Unto whom the prince of the eunuchs gave names: for he gave unto Daniel the name of Belteshazzar; and to Hananiah, of Shadrach; and to Mishael, of Meshach; and to Azariah, of Abednego.

Refusing the king's portion they thrive on vegetables and water

8 But Daniel purposed in his heart that he would not defile himself with the portion of the king's meat, nor with the wine which he drank: therefore he requested of the prince of the eunuchs that he might not defile himself.
9 Now God had brought Daniel into favour and tender love with the prince of the eunuchs.
10 And the prince of the eunuchs said unto Daniel, I fear my lord the king, who hath appointed your meat and your drink: for why should he see your faces worse liking than the children which are of your sort? then shall ye make me endanger my head to the king.
11 Then said Daniel to Melzar, whom the prince of the eunuchs had set over Daniel, Hananiah, Mishael, and Azariah,
12 Prove thy servants, I beseech thee, ten days; and let them give us pulse to eat, and water to drink.
13 Then let our countenances be looked upon before thee, and the countenance of the children that eat of the portion of the king's meat: and as thou seest, deal with thy servants.
14 So he consented to them in this matter, and proved them ten days.
15 And at the end of ten days their countenances appeared fairer and fatter in flesh than all the children which did eat the portion of the king's meat.
16 Thus Melzar took away the portion of their meat, and the wine that they should drink; and gave them pulse.

Their wisdom

17 As for these four children, God gave them knowledge and skill in all learning and wisdom: and Daniel had understanding in all visions and dreams.
18 Now at the end of the days that the king had said he should bring them in, then the prince of the eunuchs brought them in before Nebuchadnezzar.
19 And the king communed with them; and among them all was found none like Daniel, Hananiah, Mishael, and Azariah: therefore stood they before the king.
20 And in all matters of wisdom and understanding, that the king enquired of them, he found them ten times better than all the magicians and astrologers that were in all his realm.
21 And Daniel continued even unto the first year of king Cyrus.
Dan 1:1-21 (KJV)

training prophetic people to develop a strong clear prophetic flow

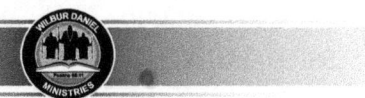

training prophetic people to develop a strong clear prophetic flow

Session Four
SCHOOL OF THE PROPHETS

THE ORIGIN

SAMUEL AND ELIJAH PROPHETIC SCHOOLS

In the year 1050 B.C., during the era of the Judges of Israel, the prophet Samuel established and conducted a training school for prophets in order to assist those called to the prophetic ministry in development and activation of their gifts.

The school was called Naioth and was located in Ramah. It was there that David found refuge from King Saul. While at Naioth, David received prophetic training, developed a sensitivity to the working of the Holy Spirit and learned how to prophesy in poetic verse. Because of this training, people have been blessed by the poetic inspiration of Psalms.

Later, Elijah, the prophet also opened schools for prophets, and after his protegee Elisha succeeded him, the demand for prophetic training required new schools to be erected.

God is once again raising up schools for prophets in order to train, equip and release His prophets and prophetic people into the world today. These prophets, and prophetic people, like John the Baptist, will prepare the way for the coming of the Lord!

SESSION FOUR SCHOOL OF THE PROPHETS

training prophetic people to develop a strong clear prophetic flow

WISDOM

> Wisdom is the principal to use for making good judgment

1 Hear, ye children, the instruction of a father, and attend to know understanding.
2 For I give you good doctrine, forsake ye not my law.
3 For I was my father's son, tender and only beloved in the sight of my mother.
4 He taught me also, and said unto me, Let thine heart retain my words: keep my commandments, and live.
5 Get wisdom, get understanding: forget it not; neither decline from the words of my mouth.
6 Forsake her not, and she shall preserve thee: love her, and she shall keep thee.

> *7 Wisdom is the principal thing; therefore get wisdom: and with all thy getting get understanding.*

8 Exalt her, and she shall promote thee: she shall bring thee to honour, when thou dost embrace her.
9 She shall give to thine head an ornament of grace: a crown of glory shall she deliver to thee.
10 Hear, O my son, and receive my sayings; and the years of thy life shall be many.
11 I have taught thee in the way of wisdom; I have led thee in right paths.
12 When thou goest, thy steps shall not be straitened; and when thou runnest, thou shalt not stumble.
13 Take fast hold of instruction; let her not go: keep her; for she is thy life.
Prov 4:1-13 (KJV)

SESSION FOUR  SCHOOL OF THE PROPHETS

training prophetic people to develop a strong clear prophetic flow

HOW TO RECEIVE A PROPHET

> The Bible states when you receive a prophet in the name of a prophet you will, receive a prophet's reward.

Matt 10:41 (KJV)

41 He that receiveth a prophet in the name of a prophet shall receive a prophet's reward; and he that receiveth a righteous man in the name of a righteous man shall receive a righteous man's reward.

The Bible said Samuel traveled in a circuit judging Israel all the days of his life. When I was reading a prophetic book, the Lord spoke to me and said the office I that I have set you in, you will function by writing prophetic curriculums and prophetical instructional material, based on what you see from traveling in a circuit from church to church in the Kingdom. Being in the midst of my people the Holy Spirit will show you where the body needs to be aligned. You then will write instructional material that will be used for training and aligning the people that I have called you to.

WAYS OF RECEIVING A PROPHET

1.) Giving to him
2.) Believe in him
3.) Receive him in your dwelling
4.) Be baptized by him (John the Baptist)
5.) Assist them in whatever business they have need of
6.) Don't be ashamed of them

Strong's Greek Number 1209
Greek word: dechomai dekh'-om-ahee
Part of Speech: v
Vine's Word(s): Accept, Accepted, Acceptable, Receive,
                Receiving,
Take
  - take 4
  - accept 2
  - take up 1 [Total Count: 59]

1) to take with the hand
1a) to take hold of, take up
2) to take up, receive
2a) used of a place receiving one
2b) to receive or grant access to, a visitor, not to refuse intercourse or friendship
2b1) to receive hospitality
2b2) to receive into one's family to bring up or educate
2c) of the thing offered in speaking, teaching, instructing
2c1) to receive favourably, give ear to, embrace, make one's own, approve, not to reject
2d) to receive. i.e. to take upon one's self, sustain, bear, endure
3) to receive, get
3a) to learn

1. Give to him
2. Believing in him
3. Receive him in your dwelling

He gives a son to the good Shunammite

8 And it fell on a day, that Elisha passed to Shunem, where was a great woman; and she constrained him to eat bread. And so it was, that as oft as he passed by, he turned in thither to eat bread.
9 And she said unto her husband, Behold now, I perceive that this is an holy man of God, which passeth by us continually.
10 Let us make a little chamber, I pray thee, on the wall; and let us set for him there a bed, and a table, and a stool, and a candlestick: and it shall be, when he cometh to us, that he shall turn in thither.
11 And it fell on a day, that he came thither, and he turned into the chamber, and lay there.
12 And he said to Gehazi his servant, Call this Shunammite. And when he had called her, she stood before him.
13 And he said unto him, Say now unto her, Behold, thou hast been careful for us with all this care; what is to be done for thee? wouldest thou be spoken for to the king, or to the captain of the host? And she answered, I dwell among mine own people.
14 And he said, What then is to be done for her? And Gehazi answered, Verily she hath no child, and her husband is old.
15 And he said, Call her. And when he had called her, she stood in the door.
16 And he said, About this season, according to the time of life, thou shalt embrace a son. And she said, Nay, my lord, thou man of God, do not lie unto thine handmaid.
17 And the woman conceived, and bare a son at that season that Elisha had said unto her, according to the time of life.

2 Kings 4:8-17 (KJV)

4.) Be baptized

Prophet John the Baptist - baptizing in the Jordan river, they received him in the name of a prophet.

5.) Assist them in whatsoever business they hath need of

1 I commend unto you Phebe our sister, which is a servant of the church which is at Cenchrea:
2 That ye receive her in the Lord, as becometh saints, and that ye assist her in whatsoever business she hath need of you: for she hath been a succorer of many, and of myself also.
3 Greet Priscilla and Aquila my helpers in Christ Jesus:
4 Who have for my life laid down their own necks: unto whom not only I give thanks, but also all the churches of the Gentiles.
   Romans 16:1-4 (KJV)

6.) Don't be ashamed of them

16 The Lord give mercy unto the house of Onesiphorus; for he oft refreshed me, and was not ashamed of my chain:
17 But, when he was in Rome, he sought me out very diligently, and found me.
18 The Lord grant unto him that he may find mercy of the Lord in that day: and in how many things he ministered unto me at Ephesus, thou knowest very well.
   2 Tim 1:16-18 (KJV)

7.) Work of labor of love

10 For God is not unrighteous to forget your work and labour of love, which ye have shewed toward his name, in that ye have ministered to the saints, and do minister.
11 And we desire that every one of you do shew the same diligence to the full assurance of hope unto the end:
12 That ye be not slothful, but followers of them who through faith and patience inherit the promises.
13 For when God made promise to Abraham, because he could swear by no greater, he sware by himself,
14 Saying, Surely blessing I will bless thee, and multiplying I will multiply thee.
15 And so, after he had patiently endured, he obtained the promise.
   Heb 6:10-15 (KJV)

8.) Be faithful & true to what you do

5 Beloved, thou doest faithfully whatsoever thou doest to the brethren, and to strangers;
6 Which have borne witness of thy charity before the church: whom if thou bring forward on their journey after a godly sort, thou shalt do well:
7 Because that for his name's sake they went forth, taking nothing of the Gentiles.
8 We therefore ought to receive such, that we might be fellow helpers to the truth.
3 John 1:5-8 (KJV)

> 1 Chron 12:32 (KJV)
> **Sons of Issachar understood the times**
> **Issacahr had four sons.**
>
> **Tola - was a judge - A judge of the tribe of Issachar who "judged" Israel twenty-three years (Jdg 10:1, 2),**

Samuel - judged Israel -
1 Samuel 1:7, 1 Samuel 1:15-17

15 And Samuel judged Israel all the days of his life.
16 And he went from year to year in circuit to Bethel, and Gilgal, and Mizpeh, and judged Israel in all those places.
17 And his return was to Ramah; for there was his house; and there he judged Israel; and there he built an altar unto the LORD.

Daniel – mean judge of God, or God is my Judge

32 And of the children of Issachar, which were men that had understanding of the times, to know what Israel ought to do; the heads of them were two hundred; and all their brethren were at their commandment.

SESSION FOUR — SCHOOL OF THE PROPHETS

training prophetic people to develop a strong clear prophetic flow

GUIDELINES FOR PROPHESYING

The Holy Bible

Commandments

Laws

Statues

Judgment

Precepts

Oracles

Offerings

Sacrifices

Feasts

Testimonies

Seasons & Times

FED BY GOD

> God may use unclean birds to feed you.
> God fed them with quails, manna,
> and your daily bread

Num 11:31 (KJV)
And there went forth a wind from the LORD, and brought quails from the sea, and let them fall by the camp, as it were a day's journey on this side, and as it were a day's journey on the other side, round about the camp, and as it were two cubits high upon the face of the earth.

Ex 16:15 (KJV)
And when the children of Israel saw it, they said one to another, It is manna: for they wist not what it was. And Moses said unto them, This is the bread which the LORD hath given you to eat.

No food, no income to buy food, God speaks to the mind of an individual to call you, take you out to purchase food.

WHEN GOD WINS YOUR CONFIDENCE

> David said, I killed a lion, and a bear, now you Goliath.

1 Sam 17:34-37

And David said unto Saul, Thy servant kept his father's sheep, and there came a lion, and a bear, and took a lamb out of the flock: And I went out after him, and smote him, and delivered it out of his mouth: and when he arose against me, I caught him by his beard, and smote him, and slew him. Thy servant slew both the lion and the bear: and this uncircumcised Philistine shall be as one of them, seeing he hath defied the armies of the living God. David said moreover, The LORD that delivered me out of the paw of the lion, and out of the paw of the bear, he will deliver me out of the hand of this Philistine. And Saul said unto David, Go, and the LORD be with thee.

SESSION FOUR — SCHOOL OF THE PROPHETS

training prophetic people to develop a strong clear prophetic flow

WHEN IT'S TIME GOD WILL HAVE THEM SEND FOR YOU

1 Sam 16:17-23

And Saul said unto his servants, Provide me now a man that can play well, and bring him to me. Then answered one of the servants, and said, Behold, I have seen a son of Jesse the Bethlehemite, that is cunning in playing, and a mighty valiant man, and a man of war, and prudent in matters, and a comely person, and the LORD is with him.
Wherefore Saul sent messengers unto Jesse, and said, Send me David thy son, which is with the sheep. And Jesse took an ass laden with bread, and a bottle of wine, and a kid, and sent them by David his son unto Saul. And David came to Saul, and stood before him: and he loved him greatly; and he became his armourbearer. And Saul sent to Jesse, saying, Let David, I pray thee, stand before me; for he hath found favour in my sight. And it came to pass, when the evil spirit from God was upon Saul, that David took an harp, and played with his hand: so Saul was refreshed, and was well, and the evil spirit departed from him.

THE PROPHETIC MINSTREL USHERS IN THE SPIRIT OF THE LORD

2 Kings 3:6-15 (KJV)
6 And king Jehoram went out of Samaria the same time, and numbered all Israel.
7 And he went and sent to Jehoshaphat the king of Judah, saying, The king of Moab hath rebelled against me: wilt thou go with me against Moab to battle? And he said, I will go up: I am as thou art, my people as thy people, and my horses as thy horses.
8 And he said, Which way shall we go up? And he answered, The way through the wilderness of Edom.
9 So the king of Israel went, and the king of Judah, and the king of Edom: and they fetched a compass of seven days' journey: and there was no water for the host, and for the cattle that followed them.
10 And the king of Israel said, Alas! that the LORD hath called these three kings together, to deliver them into the hand of Moab!
11 But Jehoshaphat said, Is there not here a prophet of the LORD, that we may enquire of the LORD by him? And one of the king of Israel's servants answered and said, Here is Elisha the son of Shaphat, which poured water on the hands of Elijah.
12 And Jehoshaphat said, The word of the LORD is with him. So the king of Israel and Jehoshaphat and the king of Edom went down to him.
13 And Elisha said unto the king of Israel, What have I to do with thee? get thee to the prophets of thy father, and to the prophets of thy mother. And the king of Israel said unto him, Nay: for the LORD hath called these three kings together, to deliver them into the hand of Moab.
14 And Elisha said, As the LORD of hosts liveth, before whom I stand, surely, were it not that I regard the presence of Jehoshaphat the king of Judah, I would not look toward thee, nor see thee.
15 But now bring me a minstrel. And it came to pass, when the minstrel played, that the hand of the LORD came upon him.

training prophetic people to develop a strong clear prophetic flow

Session Five
PROPHETS & PROSPERITY

SESSION FIVE

PROPHETS AND PROSPERITY

PROPHETS & PROSPERITY

As time passed so did the years of your accumulation of knowledge. Being a good steward has been a great asset to your wealth and prosperity. Now it's time to take all that you have learned and accomplished and turn it into gold.

IT'S GOD THAT PROSPERS YOU

Deut 8:17-18 (KJV)

17 And thou say in thine heart, my power and the might of mine hand hath gotten me this wealth.

18 But thou shalt remember the LORD thy God: for it is he that giveth thee power to get wealth, that he may establish his covenant which he sware unto thy fathers, as it is this day.

If God allow it, it's OK

(Example) I want to purchase $500.000.00 house, I have the income to afford it. I made a decision to work a second job, I started a business, and made a lot more decisions that would generate income to make payments for the house. God didn't say no to anything I've done, therefore I'll continue with my plans.

Now if God would have said no to something I would have to stop.

SESSION FIVE  PROPHETS AND PROSPERITY

training prophetic people to develop a strong clear prophetic flow

WHATEVER GOD SPEAKS,
unction or gives you faith for, do it then, find time to study, pray and research it.

2 Tim 2:15

Study to shew thyself approved unto God, a workman that needeth not to be ashamed, rightly dividing the word of truth.

The old saying is that Rome wasn't built in a day. Therefore whatever God gives you to do, start the start. Do something toward your goal everyday, take it step by step.

Matt 14:25-29

28 And Peter answered him and said, Lord, if it be thou, bid me come unto thee on the water.
29 And he said, Come. And when Peter was come down out of the ship, he walked on the water, to go to Jesus.

DON'T RE-INVENT THE WHEEL

Do what works. God said don't reinvent the wheel. What is under the sun has already been done, so take the idea and tailor it to your taste.

Eccl 1:9-10 (KJV)

9 The thing that hath been, it is that which shall be; and that which is done is that which shall be done: and there is no new thing under the sun.
10 Is there any thing whereof it may be said, See, this is new? it hath been already of old time, which was before us.

BACK INTO IT STEP BY STEP

> Whatever you do, it may take more than a day to complete. Back into it, step by step. Because step by step is the big principle of small things. Every step you take towards any given goal brings you closer to success.

—— Wilbur Daniel

SESSION FIVE — PROPHETS AND PROSPERITY

It's very important that you document what the Lord gives you. Documenting what the Lord gives you capture the very anointing that's upon the word spoken. When you document what the Lord speaks to you capture the freshness that's upon the word of the Lord. Waiting to document the word opens up possibilities to forget what God has said, and also in the anointing that he said it in.

Having faith to do a task is like having extra energy. Having faith cut through days of natural strength, allowing the spirit of faith to compel you at a faster pace with more energy. That which took you five days to accomplish in natural strength, only takes you one day in faith under the supernatural strength.

1. Why is it important to move out at the time God instructs you to do something?_____

2. Having faith for a task is like having? _____

3. Why is it important to document right away what the Lord gives you?_____

4. Is it true when you move in supernatural strength you save time?   Yes   or   No

YOU ALREADY HAVE WHAT YOU ARE LOOKING FOR.

you just have to discover it

I experienced something that made this statement true. While I was at work, I misplaced my comb. For several minutes I searched high and low with no comb to be found. It was only after I reached into my front pocket and pulled out the comb that I realized it was there the entire time.

Sometimes we are looking in all the wrong places for what we need. Re-evaluate your surroundings and look closer to the things that you own. There's treasure inside you, waiting to be unlocked.

Libraries contains books and data and a great deal of wealth of history on varieties of subjects that you can study and research.

SESSION FIVE — PROPHETS AND PROSPERITY

training prophetic people to develop a strong clear prophetic flow

God made you with everything you need to fulfill his God given plan for your life here on earth.

1. Your DNA has all the abilities it needs.

2. Your body feature has all the strengths and abilities it need.

3. The Bible says that your life is hid with Christ in God.

4. Consult Jesus for your life manual or plan for your life.

   Romans 8:26-30 (KJV)
   26 the Spirit also helpeth our infirmities: for we know not what we should pray for as we ought: but the Spirit itself maketh intercession for us with groanings which cannot be uttered. 27 And he that searcheth the hearts knoweth what is the mind of the Spirit, because he maketh intercession for the saints according to the will of God. 28 And we know that all things work together for good to them that love God, to them who are the called according to his purpose. 29 For whom he did foreknow, he also did predestinate to be conformed to the image of his Son, that he might be the firstborn among many brethren. 30 Moreover whom he did predestinate, them he also called: and whom he called, them he also justified: and whom he justified, them he also glorified.

When certain things are given to you from the Lord by revelation, knowledge, or vision, you can always ask yourself is it for know or later.

Write the vision, and make it plain upon tables, that he may run that readeth it. 3 For the vision is yet for an appointed time, but at the end it shall speak, and not lie: though it tarry, wait for it; because it will surely come, it will not tarry.
Hab 2:2-3 (KJV)

Three suggestions to help determine if it is for now or later.

- By His word
- By His will
- By His way

By His Word - A Rhema Word has been received by prophecy, preaching, or vision with a scripture even pertaining to the matter.

By His Will - It's God plan and purpose for you determine by your overall make up. These are things that you have no spiritual or natural control over. (Example) If God wanted you to be a center basketball player, He'll make you tall with a desire for basketball.

By His way - Born into a wealthy family, and your desire to give to charity,

SESSION FIVE  PROPHETS AND PROSPERITY

IS IT FOR NOW OR LATER

> God told them to gather only enough for one day's supply. If not, it would rot, but they disobeyed and gathered more. Ask yourself, when God is speaking to you, ask yourself is it for now or later?

Ex 16:15-20

And when the children of Israel saw it, they said one to another, It is manna: for they wist not what it was. And Moses said unto them, This is the bread which the LORD hath given you to eat. This is the thing which the LORD hath commanded, Gather of it every man according to his eating, an omer for every man, according to the number of your persons; take ye every man for them which are in his tents. And the children of Israel did so, and gathered, some more, some less. And when they did mete it with an omer, he that gathered much had nothing over, and he that gathered little had no lack; they gathered every man according to his eating. And Moses said, Let no man leave of it till the morning. Notwithstanding they hearkened not unto Moses; but some of them left of it until the morning, and it bred worms, and stank: and Moses was wroth with them.

THE LAW OF RECIPROCITY
The law of sowing and reaping

Giving

Luke 6:38 (KJV)
Give, and it shall be given unto you; good measure, pressed down, and shaken together, and running over, shall men give into your bosom. For with the same measure that ye mete withal it shall be measured to you again.

Tithes

Mal 3:7-10 (KJV)
10 Bring ye all the tithes into the storehouse, that there may be meat in mine house, and prove me now herewith, saith the LORD of hosts, if I will not open you the windows of heaven, and pour you out a blessing, that there shall not be room enough to receive it.

Sowing

2 Cor 9:6-7 (KJV)
6 But this I say, He which soweth sparingly shall reap also sparingly; and he which soweth bountifully shall reap also bountifully.
7 Every man according as he purposeth in his heart, so let him give; not grudgingly, or of necessity: for God loveth a cheerful giver.

Vows

Deut 23:21-23 (KJV)
21 When thou shalt vow a vow unto the LORD thy God, thou shalt not slack to pay it: for the LORD thy God will surely require it of thee; and it would be sin in thee.
22 But if thou shalt forbear to vow, it shall be no sin in thee.
23 That which is gone out of thy lips thou shalt keep and perform; even a freewill offering, according as thou hast vowed unto the LORD thy God, which thou hast promised with thy mouth.

SESSION FIVE   PROPHETS AND PROSPERITY   129

training prophetic people to develop a strong clear prophetic flow

GOD NEVER PROMOTES YOU BEYOND YOUR LAST ASSIGNMENT

Jonah was given an assignment to go to Nineveh, and cry out against it. He didn't go right away and because of his disobedience he went down, down, down. Only when he decided to obey God is when he came up, up, up.

Gen 37:28

Then there passed by Midianites merchantmen; and they drew and lifted up Joseph out of the pit, and sold Joseph to the Ishmeelites for twenty pieces of silver: and they brought Joseph into Egypt.

A PROPHET MUST UNDERSTAND THE SEASONS AND THE TIMES.

1 Chron 12:32 (KJV)
32 And of the children of Issachar, which were men that had understanding of the times, to know what Israel ought to do; the heads of them were two hundred; and all their brethren were at their commandment.

KNOW YOUR SEASON

> Whatever season it is in your life will yield the fruit of that season.

Psalms 1:3 (KJV)
And he shall be like a tree planted by the rivers of water, that bringeth forth his fruit in his season; his leaf also shall not wither; and whatsoever he doeth shall prosper.

Look back over your life and analyze where you were, and what you accomplished at that time. People are sent into your life in seasons, knowledge is exposed to you in seasons, but the most of all pay close attention to the geographical area that you are in for that season. Every area, or climate yields different fruit, know what you can produce in your climate or season

KNOW WHAT SEASON YOU ARE IN

Psalms 1:3 (KJV)
And he shall be like a tree planted by the rivers of water, that bringeth forth his fruit in his season; his leaf also shall not wither; and whatsoever he doeth shall prosper.

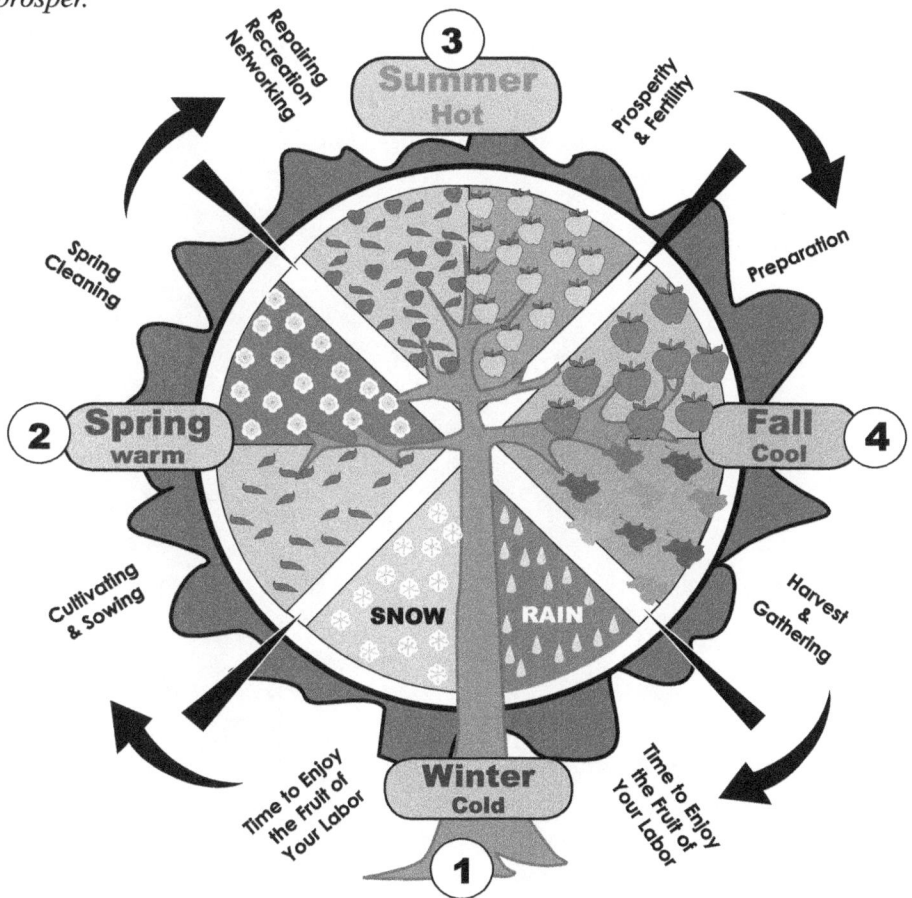

training prophetic people to develop a strong clear prophetic flow

SESSION SIX
PROPHETS & SPIRITUAL WARFARE

─ S P I R I T U A L   W A R F A R E ─

WHAT IS SPIRITUAL WARFARE ?

Spiritual warfare - is decreeing, declaring, praying, speaking and releasing God's word in the realm of the spirit over and against any negative word, curses, evil plans, plots, demonic assignments that has been released over your life, to stop brake, destroy, cancel out, abort, and reverse all that has been said or done in the realm of the spirit.

> *2 Cor 10:3-5 (KJV)*
> *3 For though we walk in the flesh, we do not war after the flesh:*
> *4 (For the weapons of our warfare are not carnal, but mighty through God to the pulling down of strong holds;)*
> *5 Casting down imaginations, and every high thing that exalteth itself against the knowledge of God, and bringing into captivity every thought to the obedience of Christ;*

The Armour

> *Eph 6:11-17 (KJV)*
> *11 Put on the whole armour of God, that ye may be able to stand against the wiles of the devil.*
> *12 For we wrestle not against flesh and blood, but against principalities, against powers, against the rulers of the darkness of this world, against spiritual wickedness in high places.*
> *13 Wherefore take unto you the whole armour of God, that ye may be able to withstand in the evil day, and having done all, to stand.*
> *14 Stand therefore, having your loins girt about with truth, and having on the breastplate of righteousness;*
> *15 And your feet shod with the preparation of the gospel of peace;*
> *16 Above all, taking the shield of faith, wherewith ye shall be able to quench all the fiery darts of the wicked.*
> *17 And take the helmet of salvation, and the sword of the Spirit, which is the word of God:*

GOD WILL SHUT THE LIONS MOUTH

Daniel 6.22

My God hath sent his angel, and hath shut the lions mouth, that they have not hurt me, for much as before him innocence was found in me; and also before thee O king, have I done no hurt.

PROTECTING YOUR ANOINTING

> Don't allow everything to enter your ear gate and eye gate. Don't allow people to make you get out of character.

— Wilbur Daniel

PUSHED INTO THE HANDS OF GOD

> Moses at the Red Sea,
> David running from Saul,
> Daniel in the lion's den,
> Elijah on Mt. Carmel and
> Gideon & Joshua

Ex 14:13-14
13 And Moses said unto the people, Fear ye not, stand still, and see the salvation of the LORD, which he will shew to you to day: for the Egyptians whom ye have seen to day, ye shall see them again no more for ever.
14 The LORD shall fight for you, and ye shall hold your peace.

In some cases the Lord will allow certain things to happen that may push us exactly where God wants us.

When the children of Israel were pushed to the red sea it was the perfect place for God to work a miracle. Sometimes the only way you will see a miracle is to be pushed to the extreme. The place of the miracle can be uncomfortable, in most cases it will be uncomfortable.

Miracles are an act of God, but having faith and trusting God is our responsibility, which can be very demanding on our prayer life.

Pushed into the hands of God, will demand a level of faith, which you have never operated in before.

KNOW YOUR STRENGTHS AND WEAKNESSES.

Judges 16:15-21

15 And she said unto him, How canst thou say, I love thee, when thine heart is not with me? thou hast mocked me these three times, and hast not told me wherein thy great strength lieth.
16 And it came to pass, when she pressed him daily with her words, and urged him, so that his soul was vexed unto death;
17 That he told her all his heart, and said unto her, There hath not come a razor upon mine head; for I have been a Nazarite unto God from my mother's womb: if I be shaven, then my strength will go from me, and I shall become weak, and be like any other man.
18 And when Delilah saw that he had told her all his heart, she sent and called for the lords of the Philistines, saying, Come up this once, for he hath shewed me all his heart. Then the lords of the Philistines came up unto her, and brought money in their hand.
19 And she made him sleep upon her knees; and she called for a man, and she caused him to shave off the seven locks of his head; and she began to afflict him, and his strength went from him.
20 And she said, The Philistines be upon thee, Samson. And he awoke out of his sleep, and said, I will go out as at other times before, and shake myself. And he wist not that the LORD was departed from him.
21 But the Philistines took him, and put out his eyes, and brought him down to Gaza, and bound him with fetters of brass; and he did grind in the prison house.

The Power of Prayer
A 21 Day Return
Daniel Prayed

10 And, behold, an hand touched me, which set me upon my knees and upon the palms of my hands.
11 And he said unto me, O Daniel, a man greatly beloved, understand the words that I speak unto thee, and stand upright: for unto thee am I now sent. And when he had spoken this word unto me, I stood trembling.
12 Then said he unto me, Fear not, Daniel: for from the first day that thou didst set thine heart to understand, and to chasten thyself before thy God, thy words were heard, and I am come for thy words.
13 But the prince of the kingdom of Persia withstood me one and twenty days: but, lo, Michael, one of the chief princes, came to help me; and I remained there with the kings of Persia.
14 Now I am come to make thee understand what shall befall thy people in the latter days: for yet the vision is for many days.
Dan 10:10-14(KJV)

INNER COUNCIL OF THE LORD

There's a road that travels around the world
There's a path that leads to a destination,
there's a bridge that crosses over water,
there's a river that flows continually,
there's a plane that can fly in midair,
and there's the realm of the Spirit
where all mysteries, wisdom, knowledge,
understanding and the perfect will
of God is revealed.
That's where I want to be

— Wilbur Daniel

Graphics by Wilbur Daniel

INNER COUNCIL OF THE LORD

After being in the inner council of the Lord (in His presence) you can give Godly counsel.

God's secret is with his secret.

Dan 2:18-23 (KJV)

18 That they would desire mercies of the God of heaven concerning this secret; that Daniel and his fellows
   should not perish with the rest of the wise men of Babylon.
19 Then was the secret revealed unto Daniel in a night vision. Then Daniel blessed the God of heaven.
20 Daniel answered and said, Blessed be the name of God for ever and ever: for wisdom and might are his.
21 And he changeth the times and the seasons: he removeth kings, and setteth up kings: he giveth wisdom unto.
22 He revealeth the deep and secret things: he knoweth what is in the darkness, and the light dwelleth with him.
23 I thank thee, and praise thee, O thou God of my fathers, who hast given me wisdom and might, and hast made
   known unto me now what we desired of thee: for thou hast now made known unto us the king's matter.

Dan 2:19-23 (KJV)

Where: In His presence. Daniel 2:27
Where: In His sight Where fresh revelation knowledge flow.
Where wisdom is: Where prophets know what time it is.

THE SPIRIT REALM

All things happens in the spirit first before they manifest in the natural.

Perfect example of this statement: God showed John visions, Daniel dreams, both saw things in the spirit that later came to pass. I encourage you to write your dreams and visions down, note and date when they come to pass.

1. What has God shown you in the spirit that has or hasn't come to pass?_____
2. Give chapter & verse of three Bible examples of God showing someone something in the spirit that came to pass in the natural.

WHAT A PROPHET DOES, HE MUST DO IN THE SPIRIT

This I say then, Walk in the Spirit, and ye shall not fulfil the lust of the flesh. Now the works of the flesh are manifest, which are these; adultery, fornication, uncleanness, lasciviousness, idolatry, witchcraft, hatred, variance, emulations, wrath, strife, seditions, heresies, envyings, murders, drunkenness, revellings, and such like: of the which I tell you before, as I have also told you in time past, that they which do such things shall not inherit the kingdom of God.

Gal 5:19-21

THE LAW OF THE SPIRIT

God is not controlled by time because the spirit realm is timeless. Sometimes God, by his Spirit, enables us to see the past, present and future happening all at the same time.

Example: I once dreamed that I came out of a door onto a busy street where there was a mixture of traffic. Horses, donkeys and mule and wagons from the 1600's; along with late model cars from the millennium were all visible on that street. My attire was casual boots, jeans, and a hat. The leather briefcase I carried seemed to be very attractive and futuristic to the by standers. I was in a time where the past, the present and the future were all happening at the same time.

—— Wilbur Daniel

THE LAW OF THE SPIRIT

Living by the law of the spirit has set me free from the law of sin and death. Romans 8:2

1 There is therefore now no condemnation to them which are in Christ Jesus, who walk not after the flesh, but after the Spirit.
2 For the law of the Spirit of life in Christ Jesus hath made me free from the law of sin and death.
3 For what the law could not do, in that it was weak through the flesh, God sending his own Son in the likeness of sinful flesh, and for sin, condemned sin in the flesh:
4 That the righteousness of the law might be fulfilled in us, who walk not after the flesh, but after the Spirit.
5 For they that are after the flesh do mind the things of the flesh; but they that are after the Spirit the things of the Spirit.
6 For to be carnally minded is death; but to be spiritually minded is life and peace.
7 Because the carnal mind is enmity against God: for it is not subject to the law of God, neither indeed can be.
8 So then they that are in the flesh cannot please God.
9 But ye are not in the flesh, but in the Spirit, if so be that the Spirit of God dwell in you. Now if any man have not the Spirit of Christ, he is none of his.
10 And if Christ be in you, the body is dead because of sin; but the Spirit is life because of righteousness.
11 But if the Spirit of him that raised up Jesus from the dead dwell in you, he that raised up Christ from the dead shall also quicken your mortal bodies by his Spirit that dwelleth in you.
12 Therefore, brethren, we are debtors, not to the flesh, to live after the flesh.

THE LAW OF THE SPIRIT

13 For if ye live after the flesh, ye shall die: but if ye through the Spirit do mortify the deeds of the body, ye shall live.
14 For as many as are led by the Spirit of God, they are the sons of God.
15 For ye have not received the spirit of bondage again to fear; but ye have received the Spirit of adoption, whereby we cry, Abba, Father.
16 The Spirit itself beareth witness with our spirit, that we are the children of God:
17 And if children, then heirs; heirs of God, and joint-heirs with Christ; if so be that we suffer with him, that we may be also glorified together.
18 For I reckon that the sufferings of this present time are not worthy to be compared with the glory which shall be revealed in us.
19 For the earnest expectation of the creature waiteth for the manifestation of the sons of God. 20 For the creature was made subject to vanity, not willingly, but by reason of him who hath subjected the same in hope,
21 Because the creature itself also shall be delivered from the bondage of corruption into the glorious liberty of the children of God.
22 For we know that the whole creation groaneth and travaileth in pain together until now.
23 And not only they, but ourselves also, which have the firstfruits of the Spirit, even we ourselves groan within ourselves, waiting for the adoption, to wit, the redemption of our body.
24 For we are saved by hope: but hope that is seen is not hope: for what a man seeth, why doth he yet hope for?
25 But if we hope for that we see not, then do we with patience wait for it.
26 the Spirit also helpeth our infirmities: for we know not what we should pray for as we ought: but the Spirit itself maketh intercession for us with groanings which cannot be uttered.
27 And he that searcheth the hearts knoweth what is the mind of the Spirit, because he maketh intercession for the saints according to the will of God.

THE LAW OF THE SPIRIT

28 And we know that all things work together for good to them that love God, to them who are the called according to his purpose.
and obtain the liberty decreed by God in advance
29 For whom he did foreknow, he also did predestinate to be conformed to the image of his Son, that he might be the firstborn among many brethren.
30 Moreover whom he did predestinate, them he also called: and whom he called, them he also justified: and whom he justified, them he also glorified.
31 What shall we then say to these things? If God be for us, who can be against us?
32 He that spared not his own Son, but delivered him up for us all, how shall he not with him also freely give us all things?
33 Who shall lay any thing to the charge of God's elect? It is God that justifieth.
34 Who is he that condemneth? It is Christ that died, yea rather, that is risen again, who is even at the right hand of God, who also maketh intercession for us.
35 Who shall separate us from the love of Christ? shall tribulation, or distress, or persecution, or famine, or nakedness, or peril, or sword?
36 As it is written, For thy sake we are killed all the day long; we are accounted as sheep for the slaughter.
37 Nay, in all these things we are more than conquerors through him that loved us.
38 For I am persuaded, that neither death, nor life, nor angels, nor principalities, nor powers, nor things present, nor things to come,
39 Nor height, nor depth, nor any other creature, shall be able to separate us from the love of God, which is in Christ Jesus our Lord.
Romans 8:1-39 (KJV)

— FEAR NOT —
Isaiah 41:10

> When God win your confidence, and you have several testimonies of what God has done for you, you can say to an individual that's being challenged with varieties of trials, FEAR NOT FOR GOD IS WITH YOU.

10 Fear thou not; for I am with thee: be not dismayed; for I am thy God: I will strengthen thee; yea, I will help thee; yea, I will uphold thee with the right hand of my righteousness.
11 Behold, all they that were incensed against thee shall be ashamed and confounded: they shall be as nothing; and they that strive with thee shall perish.
12 Thou shalt seek them, and shalt not find them, even them that contended with thee: they that war against thee shall be as nothing, and as a thing of nought.
13 For I the LORD thy God will hold thy right hand, saying unto thee, Fear not; I will help thee.
14 Fear not, thou worm Jacob, and ye men of Israel; I will help thee, saith the LORD, and thy redeemer, the Holy One of Israel.
15 Behold, I will make thee a new sharp threshing instrument having teeth: thou shalt thresh the mountains, and beat them small, and shalt make the hills as chaff.
16 Thou shalt fan them, and the wind shall carry them away, and the whirlwind shall scatter them: and thou shalt rejoice in the LORD, and shalt glory in the Holy One of Israel
Isaiah 41:10-16 (KJV)

Release a creative word over your Life.

We are seated with Jesus Christ in Heavenly places. The position we are in with Christ gives us the authority to decree and declare, and release blessing and prosperity over our lives as Christian. Now that I'm seated with Christ far above principalities and powers. I rule from a different position.

I release my name_____in the realm of the spirit, I declare and degree by the creative spoken word that the prophetic snipers, prophetic intercessors, and prayer warriors will pick me up in the realm of the spirit. I will prayer earnestly until I see a spiritual and physical manifestation take place, then I know that my assignment is complete concerning that which the Holy Spirit revealed unto me.

Jeremiah 27:18,
John 16:13,
Luke 18:7
Romans 8:26-27,
Hebrew 7:25

6 And hath raised us up together,
and made us sit together in heavenly places
in Christ Jesus

Eph 2:6 (KJV)

I decree and declare I'm blessed in the City

SESSION SIX  PROPHETS & SPIRITUAL WARFARE

training prophetic people to develop a strong clear prophetic flow

OPENED DOORS, IS IT BECAUSE OF YOU?

> Achan, Jonah, or maybe you;
> check yourself.

Jonah 1:4-7

4 But the LORD sent out a great wind into the sea, and there was a mighty tempest in the sea, so that the ship was like to be broken.
5 Then the mariners were afraid, and cried every man unto his god, and cast forth the wares that were in the ship into the sea, to lighten it of them. But Jonah was gone down into the sides of the ship; and he lay, and was fast asleep.
6 So the shipmaster came to him, and said unto him, What meanest thou, O sleeper? arise, call upon thy God, if so be that God will think upon us, that we perish not.
7 And they said every one to his fellow, Come, and let us cast lots, that we may know for whose cause this evil is upon us. So they cast lots, and the lot fell upon Jonah.

JEALOUSY, A VISION KILLER

> Don't tell them your vision, allow them to hear your testimony. Joseph had a dream that one day his brothers would give obeisance to him. When he shared his dream with his brothers, they became jealous and tried to kill the vision by selling him to a caravan going to Egypt.

Gen 37:28

Then there passed by Midianites merchantmen; and they drew and lifted up Joseph out of the pit, and sold Joseph to the Ishmeelites for twenty pieces of silver: and they brought Joseph into Egypt.

DEPRESSION...IT COMES AFTER VICTORY

> Elijah won the battle on Mount Carmel.
> Then immediately after the victory he is found
> under a juniper tree praying to die.

1 Kings 19:4-8

But he himself went a day's journey into the wilderness, and came and sat down under a juniper tree: and he requested for himself that he might die; and said, It is enough; now, O LORD, take away my life; for I am not better than my fathers.
5 And as he lay and slept under a juniper tree, behold, then an angel touched him, and said unto him, Arise and eat.
6 And he looked, and, behold, there was a cake baken on the coals, and a cruse of water at his head. And he did eat and drink, and laid him down again.
7 And the angel of the LORD came again the second time, and touched him, and said, Arise and eat; because the journey is too great for thee.
8 And he arose, and did eat and drink, and went in the strength of that meat forty days and forty nights unto Horeb the mount of God.

DON'T BE DISMAYED AT THEIR FACES

Don't let other people's disposition affect your focus. I've experienced loss and hindrances of accomplishment, because I allowed people to deter me. Their situation became my situation which affected me, don't allow this.

People will sometimes give you a hard time just to deter you from accomplishing what God, has assigned you to do.

Ezekiel 2:6

And thou, son on man, be not afraid of them, neither be afraid of them, neither be afraid of their words, thier briers and thorns be with thee, an dost dwell among scorpions: benot afraid of their words, nor be dismayed at their looks, though they be a rebellious house

SESSION SIX — PROPHETS & SPIRITUAL WARFARE

training prophetic people to develop a strong clear prophetic flow

HIDDEN BY GOD

> David in the cave of Adullam, being chased by Saul stayed there until the appointed time. Scripture states Jesus came forth at the appointed time.

1 Sam 22:1-2 (KJV)
David therefore departed thence, and escaped to the cave Adullam: and when his brethren and all his father's house heard it, they went down thither to him. And every one that was in distress, and every one that was in debt, and every one that was discontented, gathered themselves unto him; and he became a captain over them: and there were with him about four hundred men.

Dan 11:29
at the time appointed he shall return,
and come toward the south;
but it shall not be as the former,
or as the latter.

SESSION SIX  PROPHETS & SPIRITUAL WARFARE

training prophetic people to develop a strong clear prophetic flow

GOD'S WAY OF GETTING YOU OUT

Sometimes God's way of getting you out is not as pleasant as you desire. Look at the Hebrews coming out of Egypt. Paul being let down out of the window in a basket, and now you.

Ex 12:29-33
29 And it came to pass, that at midnight the LORD smote all the firstborn in the land of Egypt, from the firstborn of Pharaoh that sat on his throne unto the firstborn of the captive that was in the dungeon; and all the firstborn of cattle.
30 And Pharaoh rose up in the night, he, and all his servants, and all the Egyptians; and there was a great cry in Egypt; for there was not a house where there was not one dead.
31 And he called for Moses and Aaron by night, and said, Rise up, and get you forth from among my people, both ye and the children of Israel; and go, serve the LORD, as ye have said.
32 Also take your flocks and your herds, as ye have said, and be gone; and bless me also.
33 And the Egyptians were urgent upon the people, that they might send them out of the land in haste; for they said, We be all dead men.

2 Cor 11:33
And through a window in a basket was I let down by the wall, and escaped his hands.

SESSION SIX  PROPHETS & SPIRITUAL WARFARE

training prophetic people to develop a strong clear prophetic flow

WHEN GOD OPENS YOUR EYES

> Everyone may not see what you see.
> Elijah said," there are more with us
> than with them, Lord open my servant's eyes".

2 Kings 6:13-18

13 And he said, Go and spy where he is, that I may send and fetch him. And it was told him, saying, Behold, he is in Dothan.
14 Therefore sent he thither horses, and chariots, and a great host: and they came by night, and compassed the city about.
15 And when the servant of the man of God was risen early, and gone forth, behold, an host compassed the city both with horses and chariots. And his servant said unto him, Alas, my master! how shall we do?
16 And he answered, Fear not: for they that be with us are more than they that be with them.
17 And Elisha prayed, and said, LORD, I pray thee, open his eyes, that he may see. And the LORD opened the eyes of the young man; and he saw: and, behold, the mountain was full of horses and chariots of fire round about Elisha.
18 And when they came down to him, Elisha prayed unto the LORD, and said, Smite this people, I pray thee, with blindness. And he smote them with blindness according to the word of Elisha.

GOD BLESSES THE REAL YOU

Take a closer look at the prodigal son. He may be like you; I want it now, all that belongs to me, so life won't be so boring!" Actually you can't be like The Jones' because they obtain theirs at a soulish cost. Once you come to yourself, God will bless the real you.

People pattern their lives after other successful people, which is good if you are allowing your pattern to be you, not a cookie cutter effect of the other person you are patterning.

Have your own taste, have your own style, have your own goals, because the real you will be demonstrated through all the things you desire and accomplish.

YOUR WORK DEFINES WHO YOU ARE!

TOPICS TO STUDY FOR SPIRITUAL WARFARE

- The Power of Prayer
- Astrology
- Coven
- Occult
- Black Magic
- Extorcism
- Tools For Spiritual Warfare
- The Enemy of the Lord
- Breaking Curses
- The Apocrypha
- The Spirit of Rebellion
- Structure
- Intercessory Prayer
- Warlocks
- Divination
- Sorcery
- Poltergeist
- Yoga
- Atral Projection
- Fetish
- Lying Spirit
- Hypnosis
- Identifying your Enemy
- The Army of the Lord
- Powers & Principalities
- Flesh/Rest & Stress
- Spirits
- Order
- Enemies of the Lord
- Witches
- Mediums
- Demons
- Magic
- Fear

LET IT GO

1 Peter 5:10
10 But the God of all grace, who hath called us unto his eternal glory by Christ Jesus, after that ye have suffered a while, make you perfect, stablish, strengthen, settle you.

Let it go: things that seem or appear good but are only obstacles are weights. So let it go that the newness and freshness of God can come into your life.

Jer 33:3
God said 3 Call unto me, and I will answer thee, and shew thee great and mighty things, which thou knowest not.

Old things sometimes have a link to the past, which boggle your mind and thinking from going forward into the future. Let it go so that your mind can be clear to move into the newness that God has for you.

With one year of dejunking in North Carolina, from 12 years of collecting in Philadelphia I was able to move on to Georgia with a clear view.

— Wilbur Daniel

It's OK To Be You

Your Works Defines Who You Are!

training prophetic people to develop a strong clear prophetic flow

WDM Index

Symbols

12 Minor Prophets 84
5 Major Prophets 84
9 GIFTS OF THE SPIRIT 40

A

Among the elect 24
A Must 69
A Prophet must understand the seasons and the times. 130

B

Back into it Step By Step 122

C

Chozeh 46
Confirmation 37

D

Dabar 48
DANIEL 100
Decerning of spirits 42
Declaring 50
Decreeing 50
Depression...It comes after victory 152
Different kind of ministries 32
Don't be dismayed at their faces 153
Don't reinvent the wheel 121

E

Every Prophet must be time proven 72

F

Fed by God 112
Foresight 62

G

GOD'S GOVERMENT 25
God's ordered course 16
God's spiritual responsiblity 26
God's way of getting you out 155
God Blesses The Real You 157
God never promotes you beyond your last assignment 129
God will shut the lions mouth 135
Grace 14

H

Hidden by God 154
HOW TO RECEIVE A PROPHET 106

I

Inner Counsel of the Lord 61, 140, 141
Insight 62
In God's care 76

Is it for now or later 127
It's God that prospers You 119
I have chosen & ordained you 23

J

Jealousy, a vision killer 151
JEREMIAH 90

K

Knowing your own company 86
Know your season 51
Know your strengths and weaknesses. 138, 158

L

Let it go 159

M

Major Prophets 84
MINISTRY OF THE PROPHET 79, 80
Minor Prophets 84
Modern day prophet 68

O

Office of the prophet 74
Opened doors,Is it because of you? 150
Other than GOD know that you're in control 60

P

Perserved for purpose 29
PERSONAL MINISTRY 33
Phebe 109
PROPHECY 36
Prophecy is conditional 39
Prophet's Are GOD's Communication channel 67
Prophetic Minstrel 115
Prophets must be broken 73
Prosperity 118
Protecting Your Anointing 136
PROTOCOL of A MINISTER 31
Pushed into the hands of GOD 137

R

REALMS OF PROPHECY 43, 53
Release A creative Word over your Life 149
RESONSIBITIY 26, 27
Rhema Word 47
Ro'eh 45

S

SAMUEL 90
Samuel Anoints Saul 94
Samuel traveled in a circuit 87
Session Three 65, 103, 117
Session Two 13, 35

Spiritual Warfare 133

T

Table of Contents 5, 6, 7, 8
The creative spoken Word 53
The creative spoken word of the Lord 54
The creative spoken word of the Prophet/Prophetess 55
THE DISCOVERY PROCESS 17
The Law of the Spirit 145, 146, 147, 148
The Lord will establish the prophet 70
the modern day prophet 68
The origin 104
The process 18
The prophet'smessage 81
The SEED Group 88
The Source of revelation 44
The Spirit Realm 142
The V ision 12
THE WORK of MINISTRY 30
Tola 110

V

Vision 62

W

Whatever God speaks, ...120
What a Prophet does, he must do in the Spirit 143
What is spiritual warfare 134
When God opens your eyes 156
When GOD win your confidence 113
When it's time God will have them send for you 114
Who Can God Use 21
Why Prophet's 67
Wisdom 105
Word of knowledge 41

Y

You're here for a reason 28
You already have what you are looking for 124

Notes

Notes

training prophetic people to develop a strong clear prophetic flow

Notes

Notes

training prophetic people to develop a strong clear prophetic flow

Notes

Notes

BOOKS BY: WILBUR DANIEL

Words of Wisdom & Knowledge for Prophetic People

Words of Wisdom and Knowledge for prophetic people is a 170 page paperback book. This book is to inspire those that are seeking truth about the prophetic to stay focus.

Item No: 7316 A

Prophecy Journal

Prophecy Journal is a journal used to record prophecies and confirmation dates and time when they are fulfilled. Recording prophecies is very rewarding when you look back and reference these dates.

Item No: 7316 P

Words of Wisdom & Knowledge for Spiritual Warfare

Words of Wisdom and Knowledge for Spiritual Warfare is a small 40 page paperback booklet. This book is used to declare and decree God's Word over your life to change circumstances.

Item No: 7316 S

Dream Journal

Dream Journal is a journal used to record night dreams and visions. This paperback booklet is a great tool that's used by many to record their dreams. Also there's pages for sketching your dream.

Item No: 7316 D

VIDEOS BY: WILBUR DANIEL

The Path of Life

Item No: WDM-V01

The Law of Reciprocity

Item No: WDM-V02

Order online www.wilburdaniel.com

www.ingramcontent.com/pod-product-compliance
Lightning Source LLC
LaVergne TN
LVHW011420080426
835512LV00005B/170